A History of Fashion and Costume

Volume 4
Early America

Paige Weber

☑® Facts On File, Inc.

Early America

Copyright © 2005 Bailey Publishing Associates Ltd

Produced for Facts On File by
Bailey Publishing Associates Ltd
11a Woodlands
Hove BN3 6TJ

Project Manager: Roberta Bailey
Editor: Alex Woolf
Text Designer: Simon Borrough
Artwork: Dave Burroughs, Peter Dennis,
Tony Morris
Picture Research: Glass Onion Pictures

Printed and bound in Hong Kong

Facts On File, Inc.
132 West 31st Street
New York NY 10001

Facts On File books are available at special
discounts when purchased in bulk quantities for
businesses, associations, institutions, or sales
promotions. Please call our Special Sales
Department in New York at 212/967-8800 or
800/322-8755.

You can find Facts On File on the World Wide
Web at: http://www.factsonfile.com

Library of Congress Cataloging-in-Publication Data

Weber, Paige.
A history of fashion and costume.
    Volume 4, Early America/Paige Weber.
    p. cm.
Includes bibliographical references and
    index.
    ISBN 0-8160-5947-0
    1. Clothing and dress—South
America—History. 2. Clothing and
dress—North America—History.
3. Indians of South America—
Clothing. 4. Indians of North
America—Clothing.
    GT675.W43 2005
    391/.0098—dc 22   2004060886

The publishers would like to thank the
following for permission to use their
pictures:

Ancient Art and Architecture: 9
(bottom)
Art Archive: 8, 9 (top), 13, 15
(bottom), 16, 18, 19, 20, 21 (both),
22, 24, 26, 27, 28, 29 (top), 30, 33
(both), 34, , 36, 41 (left), 42, 48, 51
Bridgeman Art Library: 10, 11, 17, 29
(bottom), 31, 46, 53 (left)
Colonial Williamsburg Foundation: 53
(right), 56, 57, 58
Peter Newark: 41 (right), 52, 55, 59
South American Pictures: 25
Topham: 12, 37, 38, 39, 44, 45, 49
(both)
Werner Forman Archive: 6, 7, 15 (top)

Contents

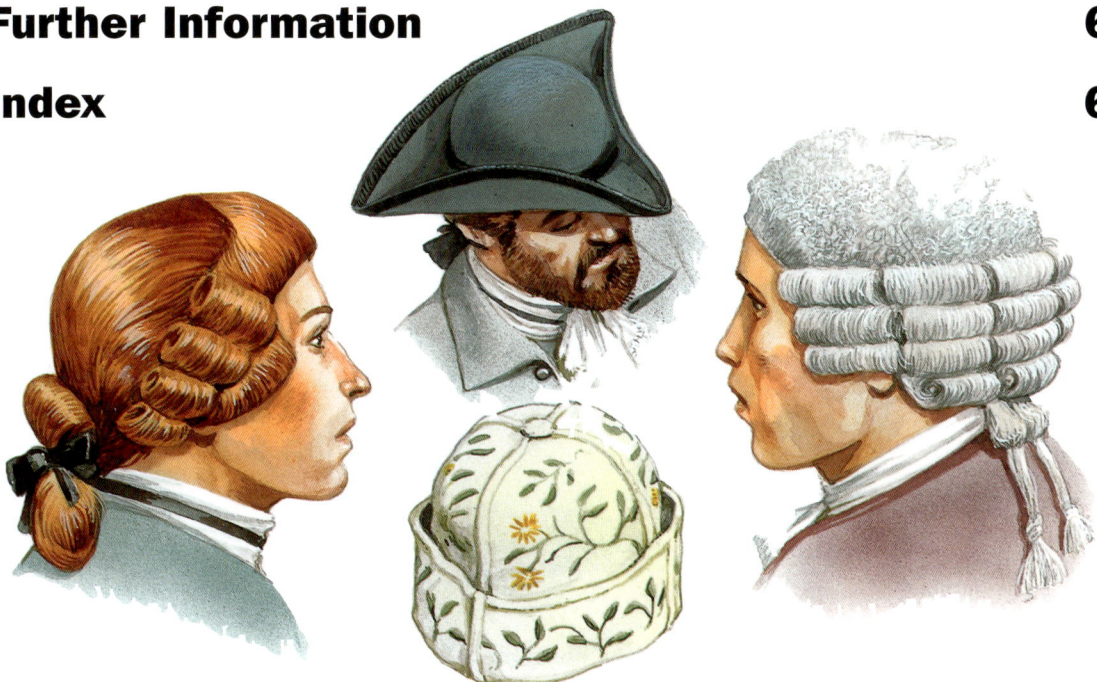

Introduction

Throughout the sixteenth and seventeenth centuries, explorers left Europe to search for westward sea routes to Asia. Instead they discovered the Americas, vast continents filled with unknown civilizations and treasures. Some of these native civilizations had developed into powerful empires.

After Christopher Columbus discovered gold on Hispaniola in 1492, Spanish and Portuguese explorers traveled to the Americas to search for more gold. With their superior steel weapons, they conquered the native peoples and took their precious treasures back to Europe.

Three great civilizations existed in Central and South America when the Europeans arrived: the Incas, the Maya, and the Aztecs. None of them had written languages, but their artwork and hieroglyphics, plus the accounts of European explorers, give us clues today about their societies and styles of clothing.

European explorers quickly understood that clothing was an important indicator of status among Native Americans. A person from any civilization could be judged instantly by the richness of his cloth, rareness of his jewelry, and magnitude of his headdress. The rulers were obvious.

English and French colonists settled in North America for many reasons. Some traded furs with the Native Americans, and others, such as the Pilgrims and Puritans, established colonies for religious freedom. Their clothing often asserted their group identities.

Though the clothing worn by these civilizations—European and Native American—differed greatly, they all shared a common interest in costume. The desire to dress up, to decorate the body, and to convey wealth and identity through clothing was common to every early American society.

Cloth and Culture in the Andes

Finely woven textiles have been central to the social, political, and economic lives of the people inhabiting the Andes mountains of South America for more than five thousand years. The Inca Empire rose to power there around 1200 CE, and at its height in the fifteenth century it ruled over a region that stretched from modern Columbia to Chile, and from the Pacific Ocean to the Amazonian rainforest. Cuzco, the central city of Inca civilization, was rich, with great buildings decorated with sheets of gold, and noblemen wearing headdresses encrusted with jewels and topped with exotic feathers.

Throughout the Inca Empire, weavings were the most important trading commodity and the most highly prized possessions. Gifts of specially woven cloth strengthened social and political ties between leaders. The Incas even worshiped a deity of textiles, Aksu Mama, to whom they made sacrifices each year.

Fibers, Dyes, and Looms

The Incas drew upon thousands of years of weaving tradition and knowledge. Brown and white cotton was cultivated in the Andes as early as 3800 BCE. Portable backstrap looms were used from 2500 BCE onwards. Camelid fibers were introduced into cloth in the ninth century BCE. In Inca society, clothes made from alpaca hair were the most common. Llama hair produced the roughest wool, and the silky hair of the wild vicuña was highly prized.

To color these yarns, the Incas used leaves, fruits, berries, lichen, tree bark, and minerals to make vivid dyes that did not fade or bleed. The cochineal insect was crushed to produce beautiful red, purple, and black dyes.

Weavers used backstrap looms to create delicate belts and headbands. Horizontal and vertical looms were used to produce larger textiles and tapestries.

Symbolism

The Incas did not have a system of written language. Instead they used symbols to convey complex information. They wove geometric patterns into their clothing to represent calendars, religious festivals,

Inca women wove cloth on backstrap looms, as shown in this sixteenth-century Peruvian illustration.

magical beliefs, and regional loyalties. For example, a diamond pattern represented Inti, the sun god. A double-headed snake pattern honored the god Amaru. The most luxurious garments were decorated with *tocapus*, small figures repeated within a larger geometric pattern. Even ordinary garments had symbolic value: farmers carried their produce in bags made of striped cloth that indicated through its patterns what was held inside.

Status and Society

Weaving was central to the economy of the Inca Empire. All people were required to pay tax to the rulers in the form of labor, called *mit'a,* often by weaving cloth. Specialist male weavers called *cumbicamayos* lived only to embroider *cumbi,* fine cloths of alpaca and vicuña fibers, which were used as diplomatic gifts by the nobility. The finest fabrics included brocades and gauzes decorated with precious metals or rare seashells. Women of all ranks spun yarns, wove cloth, and created accessories such as ponchos, belts, coca bags, and shoulder cloths. Most cloth was produced for the Inca rulers, who stored it in government warehouses until it was used as payment for soldiers or administrative officials, who turned it into clothing.

This Inca cloth, with its many colors and geometric patterns, was worn as a symbol of high social status.

Mummy Bundles

Important Incas were buried with fine, embroidered cloths. These sacred fabrics were created specifically for this purpose and were intended to accompany the wearer into the next world. Some nobles were mummified and buried in mummy bundles: mummies wrapped in layers of textiles, and topped with false heads bearing masks or wigs. These bundles would contain one large black cloth and as many other fine, colored textiles as wealth would allow.

Inca Clothing

Throughout the Inca Empire, people at all levels of society wore the same style of garments, but the cloth from which these garments were made revealed the wearers' wealth and origins. In the warm coastal lowlands, the Incas preferred cotton clothing, which kept their bodies cool. Inhabitants of the colder mountain regions wore clothes made of alpaca or llama wool. On their feet the Incas wore grass shoes or llama leather sandals bound with brightly colored wool fastenings.

This Inca nobleman wears an expensive embroidered tunic, a large headdress, and gold earrings.

The Inca government supplied some clothing to its subjects: couples were given new garments from the official warehouses when they married, and older people without families received enough clothing to survive.

Tunics and *Tocapus*

Inca men wore a loincloth, a long strip of cloth that went through the legs and wrapped around the waist to secure like a belt. In hot weather they wore this alone. On top, men wore a sleeveless, knee-length tunic made from one piece of cloth, with a slit cut through the middle to make space for the head. The waistlines of Inca tunics were often decorated with tocapus, which revealed information about the wearer, such as his wealth, birthplace, or status. Men also wore embroidered sashes around the waist. In cold weather and on formal occasions, men wore a loose cloak over a tunic, tying its two corners in front, at the neck. Instead of using pockets, men carried their tools, amulets, and coca leaves in small bags.

Warriors wore headdresses that were appropriate for their rank. Ordinary Inca helmets were round, made from wood or cane, and decorated with small braids and crests. Officers wore elaborate, feathered headdresses with ornamental badges.

Sashes and Shawls

Women wore a long, sleeveless dress that reached from the neck to the ankles and was open at the sides to ease walking. The most valuable

The Incas prized cloth decorated with repeated geometric patterns called *tocapus*.

dresses had delicate, colorful tocapus woven into the cloth around the waist. Women could also wear a sash decorated with tocapus around the waist to embellish a dress. Around the shoulders, women wore a square, draped shawl, which they fastened across the breast with a shawl pin called a *tupu* (see panel). Peasant women used these shawls to carry produce or small children.

Headbands

Ordinary Inca men wore their hair long in the back and trimmed into a neat fringe at the front. Around the head they wore a narrow, woven headband. The Incas had many different types of headbands, woolen caps, and feathered headdresses, according to their regions and status. Women wore their hair long and parted down the middle, and often twisted it into fine plaits. They cut it only at funerals. Women wore a headband similar to the men's, and noblewomen also wore a large piece of folded cloth over this. Archeologists have found bronze mirrors at Inca sites, and also bronze tweezers, which they believe were used to remove unwanted facial hair.

Shawl Pins

Inca women used long, straight metal pins called *tupu*s to fasten all of their outer garments. Tupus were made from bronze, copper, silver, or gold. One end of a tupu was sharp and the other was decorative. The decorative end could be shaped like an animal or a human figure. Most often, it took the shape of a half-moon, and was made of metal so thin and sharp that it could be used as a knife.

Manco Capac, the first Inca ruler, at the sun festival that he initiated.

Inca Aristocracy

The first Inca ruler Manco Capac is portrayed wearing enormous, spiralling, gold earrings and a richly colored robe.

The Inca rulers enjoyed the softest garments covered in *tocapus*, the most precious jewelry, and the most extravagantly plumed headdresses. Entitlement to wear embellishments like feathers, rare shells, turquoise, gold, and silver was reserved exclusively for royalty, the nobility, and the highest-ranking military officers. People from all over the Inca Empire sent tributes of rare clothing and jewelry to the emperor, and certain fabrics, feathers, and colors were claimed for his use alone. Royal and noble Inca people groomed themselves well, often bathing in private bathtubs decorated with colorful cut stones.

The Sapa Inca

The word *Inca* applies to the Inca people, and also to their emperor. The Sapa Inca, as he was known, wore a new outfit every day. He very rarely wore any garment more than once. Instead, after he wore a garment, it was stored for one year and then burned in a special ceremony. The Sapa Inca wore not only vicuña hair tunics decorated with rare shells, beads, feathers, and gold threads, but also clothes made from the rarest of fibers, such as bat hairs. Many of his clothes were woven in temples by the Virgins of the Sun, secluded women chosen for this purpose at the age of eight.

The emperor wore a royal, ceremonial headdress called a *llautu*. It was a turban of many colored folds that wrapped around his head, with a crimson-tasselled, vicuña-wool fringe

Ear Plugs

Wearing enormous plugs in the lower part of the ear, close to the lobe, was a sign of great status among Inca noblemen. Young noble boys received their first ear piercings and ear plugs during the annual Splendid Festival, when they were first recognized as adults. The materials, colors, and size of a man's ear plugs indicated his status. These ear plugs were therefore made as large as possible, and were composed of precious metals and rare stones. Through wearing them, noblemen developed stretched ears. The Spanish conquistadors called the Inca nobility *orejones*, or "big ears." Within Inca society, however, these large ears were considered prestigious.

held over his forehead by a textile band, topped with two feathers from the rare coraquenque bird. Other royal family members wore textile head–bands with royal fringes of gold and woolen tassels, but the crimson color was reserved for the Sapa Inca only.

Rare Plumes

The Inca royalty and nobility were very fond of plumed headdresses, which demonstrated to others their privileged status at a glance. Prized feathers included those of falcons, eagles, hummingbirds, herons, and egrets. The conquered tribes of the Amazon sent the Sapa Inca brilliant macaw feathers as homage, which he wore in ceremonial headdresses and fans. The feathers of the coraquenque bird were used to make only the emperor's regal headdress, and anyone caught hurting or stealing a coraquenque was immediately put to death.

Gold as the Sun

In the Inca world, gold represented the sun, and therefore the emperor. Silver symbolized the moon, and the emperor's queen. Gold and silver were used to create elaborate jewelry for the nobility. Noblemen wore intricate bracelets, disks, necklaces, pendants, and nostril rings. Women wore only necklaces and shawl pins as jewelry. The most precious stone to the Incas was blue-green turquoise, but blue lapis lazuli and black jet were also highly prized. Many precious stones and metals came from the northern edge of the Inca Empire, in modern-day Columbia.

The Incas discovered the techniques needed to work gold into decorative forms such as this necklace and brooch in the form of a llama.

Chapter 2: The Maya

Mayan Civilization

The Mayan civilization started to develop between 2000 and 1000 BCE in the Yucatán peninsula and the land covered by present-day Guatemala, Honduras, and Belize. The Maya were skilled farmers, weavers, potters, and traders, and they developed sophisticated astronomical charts, calendars, and hieroglyphic writing.

Their civilization grew in power between 250 and 600 CE, and by the early seventh century they had built dozens of city-states containing great pyramids and highly decorated stone architecture. Sometime between 650 and 900, however, the Mayan civilization went into decline. By the tenth century the Maya had largely abandoned their greatest city-states, such as Chichen Itza. Their people and culture persisted, however, in cities along the coastline. Through the sixteenth century, the Maya continued to exert a strong cultural influence on other Mesoamerican peoples through trade.

This Mayan woman wears a *huipil*, or draped blouse, over her long skirt.

The ancient zigzag symbols in this modern Mayan weaving represent lightning bolts.

Corn-Shaped Heads

The perfect Mayan head had an elongated profile that started with the end of the nose and sloped at a sharp angle up the forehead and toward the crown. Ideally, the head was shaped like an ear of corn, the Mayan staple crop. The corn god himself was represented with an elongated head. To achieve this look, they would strap two boards to the heads of newborn babies. To further enhance their profiles as adults, the Maya would use clay to shape their noses so that they appeared sleek and straight.

This stucco head of a Mayan warrior bears the ideal Mayan nose and forehead.

Text in Textiles

Like the Incas, the Maya farmed both white and light brown cotton, which they dyed and wove into colorful textiles using backstrap looms. They also used istle, fibers from the agave plant, to make rough cloth. Like other Central and South American peoples, they wove symbolism with colorful threads into their textiles, which could be read like texts and which varied according to region, family group, and tradition. Popular symbols in Mayan textiles included: two-headed animals, such as the two-headed eagle from mythology; zigzags, which represented the god of lightning; and the central mythological symbol called Yaxché, the Tree of Life.

Draped Cloth

Mayan men wore a loincloth, or *maxtatl,* a long tunic called a *xicolli,* and a cape, or *pati.* On their heads they wore a rectangular cloth folded in half diagonally and tied at the nape of the neck, known as a *tzute.* They could also wear the tzute draped decoratively over the shoulders, or as a cape during festivals. Mayan women wore a skirt with a long blouse called a *huipil* that hung down past the waist. The huipil was made from a rectangular length of cloth sewn up the sides with wide openings for the arms, and an opening in the center for the neck. Women also wore tzutes as protection from the sun, and as ornamental capes for festivals and ceremonial rituals.

Beauty Ideals

The Maya were especially interested in the human body, and they thought that certain physical traits, such as high cheekbones, represented the ideal in human beauty. The Maya also found slightly crossed eyes attractive. To give their children crossed eyes, they dangled small balls of resin between their eyes for long periods of time. The Maya decorated their teeth by filing them and then inlaying them with jade, obsidian, and other precious stones. For protection against insects and the cold, they smeared a dark clay liquid over their limbs. They also used black clay to dye their hair, and wore tattoos.

Mayan Costumes

The Maya lived according to a complex religious calendar that included many lavish seasonal rituals. During these ceremonies, the Mayan elite wore elaborate costumes that displayed their wealth and reflected their social status in the civilization's strict hierarchy. A fantastical headdress could symbolically portray the wearer's royal heritage, military achievements, or central role within a religious rite. Maya of all social classes dressed up to take part in these seasonal ceremonies. They witnessed ritual human sacrifices and watched the struggle between life and death played out through symbolic ball games.

Heads of Society

The Mayan aristocracy wore long robes and cloaks decorated with richly woven patterns and colorful knots, fringe, and feathers from sacred quetzals and other rare birds. Royal men wore clothing and sandals made

Mayan aristocrats wearing large jewelry and elaborate headdresses. Their servant carries a fan to keep them cool.

This painted vessel shows a ball player wearing thick padding to protect his body during the game.

The Ball Game

Many Mesoamerican societies played a ball game that held great significance, not just as a sport but as a ritualistic way of settling disputes. The Maya inherited this game from their predecessors the Olmecs, and they considered it so important that they built ball courts in all but the smallest towns. Players were divided into two teams, and the game involved hitting a large, heavy rubber ball across the court and into high hoops. To play, they wore a loincloth with a thick padded belt to protect the waist and hips. They also wore padding on their forearms and knees, at the sides of the body, to protect themselves from injury when diving to the ground. Players also wore large headdresses and decorative chest ornaments. To the Maya, the game represented the struggle between the forces of life and death, and the losers were often decapitated.

from jaguar pelts. Royal women wore long dresses with woven belts that displayed noble insignia. Royal Maya of both sexes wore feathered headdresses in extravagant shapes, such as a pagoda, a shell, or a bunch of fruit. The larger the headdress, the greater the status of the wearer. Rich men also wore lots of jewelry, including pectorals and leg and arm bands of jade, gold, and rare sea shells. Men pierced their ears, noses, and lips to hold large rings and studs. The richest aristocrats had servants who carried large feathered fans to keep them cool.

Mayan Warriors

Warriors belonged to the elite of Mayan society, and the highest-ranking warriors sometimes wore jaguar pelts like royalty. Going into battle, a Mayan warrior wore quilted cotton body armor, a square chest ornament, and a battle headdress intended to frighten his opponents. He carried a sharp stone spear, mace, ax, or arrows, and a wooden shield decorated with tassels. The Maya often went to war with the objective of finding victims for sacrificial rituals. During these rituals, warrior chiefs wore tunics decorated with symbols relating to the occasion, and elaborate pectoral jewelry depicting animals and humans.

Half Humans, Half Animals

The Maya held many ceremonies that involved human sacrifice, as a payment to the gods in return for favors such as rain, a good harvest, or

victory over enemies in battle. Many of the Mayan gods were depicted as half human and half animal. When the Mayan royals dressed for these sacred rituals, they often wore hybrid costumes and headdresses representing bird-men, feline men, reptilian men, and other monstrous creatures. Other Maya would be chosen to represent particular gods by dressing in costumes representing them during the festivals.

The enormous headdress worn by the King of Copan in this statue indicates his royal status.

Chapter 3: The Aztecs

Rulers of Mexico

In the thirteenth century, groups of hunter–gatherers known as the Mexica took over the cities of the great Toltec civilization in the Valley of Mexico. There they settled, combining their own cultural traditions with those of the Toltecs, and creating the early Aztec civilization. They founded the city of Tenochtitlán, modern Mexico City, on a lake island in 1325. Tenochtitlán became the seat of the emperor and the heart of the Aztec Empire.

This twentieth-century mural painting by Diego Rivera shows ancient Aztecs in typical clothes at the great market of Tenochtitlán.

Over the course of the next hundred years, the Aztecs gained complete power over the region and ruled over lands as far as the border of present-day Guatemala. The Aztec Empire was destroyed by the Spanish conquistadors in the early sixteenth century.

Aztec Civilization

At the height of their civilization, the Aztecs developed advanced art, literature, pictorial writing, music, and scientific knowledge. They lived within a strictly hierarchical society, with an emperor at the top, then royalty, nobility, priests, and warriors. Below them were craftsmen, farmers, and laborers, with slaves at the bottom. The right to wear certain precious ornaments and fine clothing was reserved by law for royalty and the nobility. The penalty for dressing better than your station could be death.

The Aztecs worshiped many gods. Some Aztec gods had been known in Mexico for centuries, and others were adopted from the religions of tribes the Aztecs had conquered. Agriculture was very important to them, and they kept carved stone calendars to plan the seasonal rituals that they hoped would bring them good harvests. Many of their religious rites involved human sacrifice, which they believed kept nature in balance.

Conquest and Culture

Aztec warriors aimed to capture outlying towns and to force the

Montezuma's Wardrobe

Montezuma came to power in 1503 and was the last ruler of the Aztec Empire before the Spanish came to Mexico in 1519. Like previous emperors, he had a godlike status and was considered too important for his feet to touch the earth. So the Aztecs spread cloaks on the ground wherever he walked. Montezuma owned many fantastic and opulent cloaks, including one made from white duck feathers with a wolf's head pattern; and another one lavishly covered with rare quetzal feathers. Montezuma cleaned himself frequently in steam baths, as it was important that he and his clothing remained spotlessly clean. Turquoise was considered a royal stone, and Montezuma's imperial diadem was encrusted with turquoise.

As the emperor, he was the only Aztec allowed to wear a turquoise nose ornament.

The coronation of the Aztec emperor Montezuma II.

conquered people to pay tribute to the empire. As the Aztecs conquered neighboring tribes, they absorbed their cultures into their own civilization. The conquered tribes paid the Aztec rulers with gold, precious stones, rare feathers, cotton, and elaborate costumes in return for their spared lives. Aztec merchants traveled far to spy on foreign tribes and report back to Tenochtitlán with news of their wealth, often perceived through fine clothing and jewelry. If a foreign tribe refused to trade goods with the Aztecs, war and often conquest followed.

Aztec Dress

This scene from Diego Rivera's mural depicts ordinary Aztecs working in Tenochtitlán at the height of the Aztec Empire.

Living in the hot, dry central plains of Mexico, the Aztecs wore loose, flowing clothing made of fabric that breathed and kept them cool. Richer members of society wore cotton imported from the warm coastal regions, while the poor wore local maguey cactus fiber cloth. The Aztecs loved finery, and they decorated themselves and their clothing with animal and floral patterns, fur, feathers, fringe, precious stones, and seashells, especially during festivals.

Materials and Dyes

Unlike the Incas, the Aztecs did not farm camelids for wool. In their hot climate they preferred to farm soft cotton along the Pacific coast, and the common maguey cacti, which produced a rough clothlike linen.

Grass Sandals

Ordinary Aztecs went barefoot over the hot, dry ground. Soldiers and wealthy people, however, wore sandals made from leather or vegetable fibers such as corn husks, grass, or yucca. More expensive sandals were decorated with black, brown, red, or yellow designs woven through with dyed fibers. Leather or fiber straps held the sandals in place between the big and first toes. The most complicated sandals had long leather straps that wrapped around the leg from the ankle to the knee.

Women spun the yarn, wove it into cloth on backstrap looms, and embroidered it with cactus needles.

The Aztecs loved colorful clothing and used many different dyes. The mora tree produced yellowish-green dye, and acacia leaves made blue dye. Molluscs from the Pacific coast yielded purple dye. The deep, crimson dye produced from the crushed bodies of cochineal insects was highly prized. The Aztecs farmed cochineal insects in their natural habitat, prickly pear cacti. Aztec women used colorful yarns to weave designs representing butterflies, snakes, flowers, conch shells, and geometric shapes into the finest cloth for the nobility.

Men's Clothing

The loincloth was the basic item of clothing for all Aztec men. A loincloth was a long strip of fabric that passed between the legs, wrapped around the waist, and then knotted so that the ends hung down a short length in front and behind. Poor men often wore loincloths made of white maguey fiber cloth. Noblemen wore soft cotton loincloths embroidered with patterns that showed their status.

Over their loincloth, richer men wore a rectangular cloak tied into a knot on the right shoulder. The nobility wore colorful cloaks woven with intricate patterns and trimmed with fur, shells, feathers, or precious stones. The richest men wore several of these fine cloaks at the same time.

As Aztec clothing had no pockets, men wore small pouches over their shoulders to carry tools and coca leaves to chew.

Women's Clothing

The basic garment for an Aztec woman was an ankle-length skirt held in place at the waist by an embroidered belt. Ordinary skirts were made from plain, white cloth, but rich women wore skirts embroidered with designs of fishes, birds, leaves, and flowers. Over her skirt, a noblewoman wore a loose, straight shirt sewn up at the sides and decorated along the neck and the lower border.

To make themselves more attractive, Aztec women often colored their faces with ocher powder and dyed their hair with indigo to make it glossy and black. Young women wore their hair straight and long, while married women looped their hair up into two tufts at the sides that looked like horns.

This codex drawing shows an Aztec man dressed in a rectangular cloak and an Aztec woman dressed in a long skirt with a loose shirt.

Jewelry and Decoration

Aztec men and women loved to show off by dressing up in jewelry, carrying fans, and wearing headdresses. They prized jade and turquoise above all other stones, and used gold, silver, and rare shells to make necklaces, pendants, bracelets, rings, brooches, and chest ornaments. Aztec men pierced their ears, noses, and lips to hold large stone and metal jewelry. Feathers gathered from the distant tropical regions of the Aztec Empire decorated elaborate royal headdresses, fans, and shields. Aztec metal and feather craftsmen belonged to important guilds and lived in exclusive communities under the perceived protection of their own deities.

Precious Stones and Metals

The Aztecs valued turquoise and jade from western Mexico more highly than any other material including gold. Only the Aztec emperor was allowed to wear a nose ornament made from turquoise. Jade and turquoise pieces were placed in mosaic patterns on gold crowns, helmets, ear pieces, and bracelets. Aztec jewelers also used amber, emeralds, obsidian, rock crystal, amethysts, and rare shells to create amulets worn for good luck.

Aztec smiths worked with gold from the Pacific coast, silver from Oaxaca, and copper, which they mixed with gold to create a cheaper alloy called *tumbaga*. Goldsmiths devised a clever casting technique in which wax held the gold's shape during the casting process, then melted away to leave hollow gold pieces, which could be shaped like shells, bells, frogs, or other rounded forms from nature.

Body Piercing

An Aztec nobleman experienced his first body piercing during childhood, when his ears were fitted with tiny studs. Gradually these studs were replaced with larger ear ornaments until his ears had been stretched wide enough to hold thick rods that displayed large, heavy disks. Men also

The Mixtecs, who lived at the southern edge of the Aztec Empire, were highly skilled in creating intricate gold artworks like this pendant showing the god Xipe.

pierced their noses at the nostrils to hold nose studs, and through the bridge to hold rods of gold or precious stones. Through one or two pierced holes in their lower lips, men wore labrets—pieces of gold, stone, or shell shaped like eagles, serpents, and other animals.

This shield, made of gold and feathers, was owned by the Aztec emperor Montezuma II. The central figure might be a coyote or a mythical creature.

Featherwork

The colourful, exotic birds that lived in the remote, tropical regions of the Aztec Empire yielded feathers that the nobility wore in their clothing and accessories. The Aztecs prized eagle, parrot, and hummingbird feathers, and considered the bright green feathers of the quetzal bird sacred. Quetzal feathers represented wisdom and fertility, and were added to the emperor's headdresses. Feather merchants brought rare feathers to Tenochtitlán, where the

Honored Jade

Jade was so highly prized by the Aztecs that the Aztec word for jade, *chalchihuitl,* referred to the stone and also to anything precious. To the Aztecs, jade represented water, a symbol of life and purity, and they believed that it held medicinal powers. They carved jade to create necklaces, bracelets, and ceremonial masks. When a rich person died, mourners placed jade beads in his or her mouth to symbolize eternal life after death. When the Aztec emperor Montezuma met Hernan Cortes, he gave him three jade beads that were worth more than 100 pounds of gold to the Aztecs.

featherworkers made fans, shields, armbands, sashes and tassels for the royal family and aristocracy. The featherworkers also created stylish feathered tunics and cloaks, and knotted quills onto cloth backings to create spectacular headdresses for the nobility and priests.

Wealthy Aztec men wore pectoral ornaments such as this one, made from gold and turquoise around 800–1500 CE.

Aztec Warriors

The last Aztec emperor Cuauhtemoc wearing a hairstyle to reflect his status.

Soldiers in the Aztec Empire did not wear standardized uniforms. Each warrior outfitted himself in items of clothing and ornaments that not only protected his body but also displayed his officially acknowledged rank and military achievements. A successful warrior earned the right to wear particular styles of helmets, insignia, patterned cloth, lip and ear ornaments, and even hairstyles. A warrior's military rank and record for capturing prisoners was therefore immediately recognizable on the battlefield and at special ceremonies. If a warrior dressed in clothing of a higher rank than he was entitled, he could be put to death. Aztec warriors were not paid in money, but those who distinguished themselves in battle received gifts of clothing and jewelry from the aristocracy.

Knightly Orders

When an Aztec warrior had captured more than four prisoners, he could join one of the highest-ranking orders of knights. These were the Eagles, the Jaguars, and the Arrows. Knights wore costumes that were intended to give them the appearance, strength, and abilities of wild animals. An Eagle Knight wore a helmet shaped like an eagle's head with an open beak, through which his face appeared. A Jaguar Knight wore a suit of jaguar or ocelot skins that fitted tightly over his torso, legs, and arms. The fierce head of the animal covered his own head, and his face showed through the sharp teeth.

Lower Ranks

Captains of the lower ranks sported wood or leather helmets carved into menacing shapes. They decorated their helmets and clothing with heraldic badges. Each regiment had

Warrior Hairstyles

The hair of an Aztec warrior conveyed his status and accomplishments in battle at one glance. A new recruit to the military, at the age of between ten and fifteen, shaved his head and wore a single pigtail at the back. When he had taken his first prisoner in battle, the soldier could remove this pigtail and replace it with a new hairstyle of a single lock of hair hanging over his right ear. If the recruit failed to capture a prisoner in four successive military campaigns, however, he was forced to wear a single pigtail forever—a humiliating fate. Knights ranked just below the Eagle Knights were called the "shorn ones" for their distinctive shaved heads and single, upright locks of hair that waved intimidatingly in battle. A messenger reporting war news back to Tenochtitlán bound his hair up if reporting a victory, but wore it loose over his face if the news was bad.

its own emblems, and successful warriors sewed these onto their body armor for identification. At military ceremonies, the captains wore leather collars decorated with rare shells, and lip ornaments in the shapes of their insignia. New soldiers wore plainer lip ornaments made from common shells or metals shaped like disks.

Body Armor

Aztec body armor needed to be light, flexible, and suitable for Mexico's hot climate. It also needed to protect the wearer against sharp obsidian arrows and javelins. Cotton,

a lightweight but strong fabric that lets air flow through easily, was supplied to Tenochtitlán from the coastal regions to make war garments. The most common battle garment was a one-piece suit of armor that combined a sleeveless top with knee-length trousers and fitted tightly around the body. Ordinary soldiers wore armor made from plain, white cotton, but soldiers of higher ranks decorated their outfits with colorful embroidered emblems. Warriors from the nobility sometimes added large, gold chest and back plates on top of their cotton armor.

These Aztec soldiers belong to the highest-ranking orders of knights: the Eagle Knight on the left is dressed in feathers and a beaked headdress; and the soldier on the right, wearing a suit of jaguar skins, is a Jaguar Knight.

Ritual and Sacrifice

Costumes played a central role in the Aztecs' religious and civil ceremonies. The Aztecs believed in many gods, each of whom wore distinctive ornaments and articles of clothing. The earth goddess Coatlicue wore a skirt of poisonous snakes. The rain god Tlaloc wore a mask that ringed his eyes, a fringe over his mouth, and clothes that were the blue-green color of water.

The Aztecs believed that in order to have rain, a good harvest, or success in battle, they needed to offer sacrifices of blood and human victims to the gods. Many Aztec ceremonies involved this ritual. At the end of the Aztec year, priests dressed in the costumes of the gods for a processional ceremony. The Aztec emperor dressed in sumptuous, symbolic costumes that reinforced people's perception of him as semi-divine. Ordinary Aztecs wore body paints and their finest clothing and accessories.

Blood and Bones

Aztec priests used human blood as an offering to the gods, and often practiced ritual human sacrifice. They lived and dressed in a terrifying manner. Priests fasted often and they were very thin. They never washed and never cut or combed their hair. Using cactus spines, they took blood from their own ears for religious offerings, and so their ears and hair were caked with blood. The priests covered themselves in long, black or dark green robes embroidered with patterns of human bones and skulls. During rituals, they painted their entire bodies with black paint that might have contained a drug.

Warrior Priests

Priests could also serve a religious function in the military, where they formed a separate class of warrior priests. These warrior priests could be identified in battle by the red paint on the sides of their heads. One of

Aztec priests dressed in special, symbolic costumes to enact their frequent rituals of human sacrifice.

Bound Together

On her wedding day, an Aztec bride put on ocher paste makeup to give her skin a yellow tone, and covered her arms and legs with red feathers. She then led a procession to the groom's house, where the groom waited for her on a ceremonial mat. The couple then sat together and anointed each other with perfume. The bride's mother gave the groom a new loincloth and cloak, and the groom's mother gave the bride a new skirt and blouse. Then the wedding ceremony official tied the man's cloak to the bride's blouse to symbolize their joined lives. At that moment they became man and wife.

several uniforms that they could wear was the Huaxtec uniform of a suit that covered the body and a conical hat in red, blue, yellow, green, white, or black, with white dots like stars.

Seasonal Ceremonies

At the spring festival for the god Xipe Totec, priests sacrificed and skinned human victims, then dyed their skins yellow and wore them, calling them *teocuitlaquemitl,* or "golden clothes." These skins were to symbolize the new "skin" of fresh grass upon the earth. At the Volador festival, four men dressed as birds attached themselves to ropes and jumped from a high pole, then spun around the pole to represent the circuit of the sun. For the Feast of Tezcatlipoca, the priests chose one young, unblemished man each year. This man dressed as the god for one year, wearing expensive clothing with black face paint, gold bracelets, and bells on his legs. At the year's end, a priest sacrificed him to the god, and the other Aztecs put on new clothes to mark the start of a new year.

This is how the Aztecs depicted Tlaloc, their rain god.

The Spanish Conquistadors

In 1492 the explorer Christopher Columbus sought a new, westward sea route from Europe to Asia. He landed on the Caribbean island of Hispaniola. There he encountered a native tribe, the Taino, who wore gold nose ornaments. Columbus reported this sighting of gold to his sponsors, the Spanish king and queen. The desire for more gold from this New World led to further Spanish exploration and colonization, and eventually to the conquest and destruction of the Aztec and Inca civilizations.

This portrait of Hernan Cortes shows him in parade armor, wearing a coat of arms and the regalia of a marquis.

In the sixteenth century many Spanish adventurers and soldiers, such as Hernan Cortes and Francisco Pizarro, set out for the New World to find the treasures held by unknown civilizations and bring them back to the Spanish court. Known as the conquistadors, or conquerors, they wore a combination of metal armor, mail, and ordinary European clothing. Eventually the conquistadors adopted the more flexible, quilted body armor worn by their Aztec and Inca opponents, and mixed this with their other clothing.

Seafaring Clothes

During the long journey across the Atlantic Ocean, men sometimes applied their sewing skills, used to repair sails, to embroider their own clothing. They also made hats, sandals, and slippers from ropes, and pouches from leather scraps. They wore coarse cotton trousers, linen shirts, loose-fitting jackets, and neck

Conquistador Helmets

The conquistadors are best recognized today by their distinctive metal helmets. They actually wore a variety of helmet styles made from solid iron or even mail, but the most famous style is the *morion*, which was popular in the second half of the sixteenth century. Made from two iron plates riveted together, the morion helmet was shaped to deflect blows. Its broad, curved brim met in points at the center front and center back, and its comb was high. A leather chin strap held it in place. Inside, it had a leather band to which a comfortable lining was stitched.

The *morion* helmet was the most popular style of Spanish helmet in the late sixteenth century.

A Spanish soldier of the sixteenth century wore steel armor, chain mail, and short, puffed breeches.

scarves to keep comfortable and warm on board ship.

Spanish colonists traveled to the new lands in South and Central America wearing the type of clothing worn at home in Spain. Often, though, they found that their familiar clothes were impractical in their new environments, which might be hot, humid, cold, or inhabited by dangerous animals and insects. As there were few women living in the Spanish colonies, men had to learn how to mend and sew their own garments.

Córdoba and the Maya

In 1517 the Spanish captain Fernandez de Córdoba and his conquistadors became the first Europeans to meet the Maya, whose civilization by then was in decline. They met at the northern tip of the Yucatan peninsula, along the coastline. A group of Mayan merchants approached the Spanish ship to trade beads, jewelry, and clothing. Through this encounter, Córdoba gained some gold pieces

that the Maya had traded with people living to the west, in Mexico.

The Spanish had not heard of the Aztecs before, but this initial evidence of gold spurred them on to travel westward, seeking more gold in the center of the Aztec Empire. The fierce Mayan warriors were hostile to the Spanish, but their stone-edged swords and axes were no match for the Spanish steel swords and harquebuses (early portable guns). By the 1540s the Spanish had gained control over the Mayan regions, though the Mayan people and their culture have survived to this day.

Clash of Cultures

When the Spanish conquistador Hernan Cortes confronted the Aztec emperor Montezuma II in 1519, the two rulers had almost no knowledge of each other's civilizations. The conquistador Francisco Pizarro met the Sapa Inca Atahuallpa in 1532 with little more information. In such extraordinary situations, both sides judged the others quickly on the basis of obvious information, such as physical appearance and clothing. This information helped to identify power and wealth, but it could also be misleading. The Aztecs believed at first that the white-skinned and bearded Spanish were gods, not men. Gold treasures given to the Spanish by the Aztecs and the Incas did not appease them, but only encouraged them to demand more gold treasures.

Cortes and Montezuma

Montezuma heard reports in 1519 of bearded white men in black robes who had landed in ships and who were approaching the heart of the Aztec Empire. This description and the date of their landing matched an Aztec legend, and Montezuma concluded that the god Quetzalcoatl had returned, in the form of Cortes, to rule his empire. Montezuma sent gifts of the god's costumes to the Spanish, but the conquistadors continued to march onward.

When Cortes arrived in Tenochtitlán, Montezuma greeted him dressed in his most regal costume, and gave him gifts of gold necklaces, jewels, feathered headdresses, and several thousand finely woven garments. In Aztec society, this was a symbol of Montezuma's power. For the Spanish, the sight of such riches merely whetted their appetites for more. The Spanish captured Montezuma. They defeated the Aztec Empire after a long siege of Tenochtitlán, which ended on August 13, 1521.

Pizarro and the Incas

The conquistadors first encountered the Incas and their treasures in 1527. They brought Inca gold and silver jewelry, precious jewels, and

Gold and Silver

The Spanish Empire grew very rich from the gold and silver taken from the Aztecs and Incas. They stripped all of their temples and palaces of precious metal objects and set up foundries to melt the jewelry, statues, cups, and other treasures down into ingots. The Spanish created the colony of Lima on the coast of modern Peru for this purpose. Between 1500 and 1650, the Spanish shipped 181 tons of gold and 16,000 tons of silver from the Americas back to Europe. As a result, very few pieces of Aztec and Inca artistry survive today.

Gold lip ornament.

This portrait shows the conquistador Francisco Pizarro dressed in thick, steel Spanish armor.

Armor in Action

embroidered clothing back to the Spanish king, who subsequently financed a conquest. Francisco Pizarro marched high into the Andes mountains in 1532 with an army of hundreds of Spanish soldiers and rebellious native warriors. Pizarro's men, unused to the altitude and cold, were inappropriately dressed in light cotton clothes. When the Spaniards reached the capital, the Incas were amazed by their appearance and weapons. With the use of firearms, Pizarro's forces quickly captured the Sapa Inca Atahuallpa and conquered the Inca Empire.

The Aztec and Inca weapons and armor were primitive compared to those of the Spanish. The Native American people had never seen horses, cannons, or guns before. The smoke and fire that burst forth from the Spanish weapons terrified them. They were used to killing their enemies at close range with stone weapons. The Spanish, dressed in steel armor and firing harquebuses, did not take long to conquer the Aztec and Inca Empires.

Atahuallpa, the last Inca ruler, was quickly captured by Pizarro's small army.

Colonial Spain

Pedro de Alvarado, a superior officer in Cortes's army, dressed in an expensive Spanish doublet, ruff, and breeches for this portrait.

Reports of the gold, silver, and precious jewels found in Central and South America drew more than 250,000 Spanish people to the American colonies in the sixteenth century. St. Augustine, founded in 1565, was the first permanent European colony on North American soil, and the Spanish had established 121 towns in the Americas by 1574. The Spanish divided the New World into two viceroyalties: New Spain covered Mexico, Central America, and the Caribbean islands; and Peru extended to all of South America except Brazil.

Most of the colonists were young, single men from the middle classes, though the colonial rulers were aristocrats. Spanish women began arriving too, and by the 1570s they comprised one third of the colonists. Most male colonists took partners from the native population, producing children of mixed race known as mestizos. Spanish colonial society produced a class system based on race, with pure Spanish at the top, followed by people of mixed race,

Buccaneers

During the seventeenth century, English, French, and Dutch pirates, known as buccaneers, cruised the Caribbean, attacking Spanish ships loaded with treasure. These men were originally lone hunters living in the abandoned island settlement of Hispaniola. They dressed in uncured animal skins, with cloths wrapped around their heads like turbans. They joined forces when the Spanish tried to drive them away, and started to wear seafaring clothing (see page 26). According to legend they invented the cutlass, a short, broad sword. However, it is more likely that Barbary pirates from the Mediterranean coast of North Africa introduced cutlasses to Hispaniola. They probably developed the cutlass from a similar kind of North African Islamic weapon. The cutlass was particularly well-suited to fighting in cramped quarters aboard ships.

and with natives and slaves at the bottom.

Doublets and Display

At first, the Spanish colonies were military outposts, and civilians and soldiers wore the same protective style of clothing. Spanish colonial men wore a mixture of military and civilian clothing that was popular in sixteenth-century Spain. Most clothing was made from dark fabrics, which could be decorated with gold, pearls, and precious stones.

In battle and on formal occasions, a man wore a doublet, a close-fitting jacket with a short, upright collar that fastened in front with hooks, straps, or buttons. The doublet could have attached or detachable sleeves, and was often longer in the front than in the back. Men wore doublets over mail or under armor. If unarmed, men might wear a short, circular cloak instead. Padding at the front of the doublet to create a bulge over the stomach was fashionable.

Under the doublet, men wore a linen shirt with narrow frills or ruffs. Short, puffed breeches were popular at first, but sleeker styles of tight hose made from cloth later became the prevailing style.

Priests

Spanish missionaries came to the American colonies to convert the native people to Christianity. Priests wore long robes that tied at the waist with a simple belt. They regarded the Native Americans as heathens, and

destroyed their religious structures and sacred items. The priests ordered the Native American men to wear Spanish clothing, and the women to cover their bodies from head to foot. When Spanish priests encountered the conquered Aztec priests, they forced them to wash and cut their blood-caked hair.

Arms and Armor

A full suit of sixteenth-century Spanish steel armor weighed seventy-six pounds (34.5 kg) and was very uncomfortable to wear in the American heat and humidity. A typical suit included a helmet, gorget for the neck, breast plate, back plate, gauntlets for the hands and wrists, cuisses and greaves for the thighs and shins, poleyns for the knees, and sabatons to protect the feet. Inside the suit, a soldier might also wear a mail shirt or skirt. Soldiers going into battle carried harquebuses, broadswords, hand axes, halberds, and leather-covered wooden shields.

Double wedding between two Inca women and two Spanish men. All wear European costume.

31

The Land of Brazil

The first Europeans to encounter the tropical forests of Brazil were led by the Portuguese explorer Pedro Cabral in 1500. Cabral and his men did not find any evidence of gold, silver, or jewels, but they did find brazilwood, which could yield a reddish dye much valued in Europe. Cabral claimed the land for Portugal. The French tried to capture the brazilwood trade in the 1520s, and in response, the Portuguese king founded a well-armed colony at São Vicente in 1532. The Portuguese had heard stories about the gold and silver found by the Spanish in South America, and they hoped that Brazil would yield similar treasures. When gold was discovered in southern Brazil in the 1690s, around 300,000 Portuguese colonists moved there in the hopes of making their fortunes.

Brazilwood

Throughout the Middle Ages, Europeans called red dyes produced from Asiatic and African trees by the name *brasil*, from the Germanic word *brasa,* meaning "glowing coals." Before the discovery of brazilwood in South America, these dyes were imported in small quantities from the Orient and used to dye textiles. The South American brazilwood tree yields both red and yellow permanent dyes. The Portuguese colonists exported brazilwood to Europe and made great fortunes. King Emanuel of Portugal named the South American country Brazil after this, its most valuable export.

El Dorado

Many expeditions into the interior of Brazil were driven by the legend of El Dorado, or "The Golden Lord." When the Spaniards explored the interior of modern Venezuela and Columbia in 1541, they encountered natives who told them the legend of a great prince who dressed in a fine powder of gold dust each day. The natives were vague about El Dorado's location, however. The Portuguese settlers, who heard the legend from the Spanish, launched many expeditions into the Brazilian interior in search of El Dorado. The Golden Lord remained elusive, however, and it would be two centuries before they found gold. The term *El Dorado,* which means "golden thing" in Spanish, was later applied to any place where gold was found.

"El Dorado" is dressed by his attendants in a fine powder of gold dust

The Amazonian People

The native people of the Amazon, the world's largest tropical rainforest, lived in small villages of fewer than a thousand people, or wandered as hunter–gatherers. The climate in the Amazon brought heavy rains and hot, steamy weather, and so the Amazonian people wore very little clothing. Instead, they used tattoos and body paint all over their bodies. Basic garments consisted of a small grass or cotton loincloth for a man or a short skirt that wrapped around the waist for a woman. They used the brilliantly colored feathers of tropical birds to create large ceremonial headdresses. Men and women wore feathers and leaves in their ears, and bead necklaces. Both sexes pierced their lower lips, and wore wooden disks or thin sticks through them as ornaments.

Bandeirantes

Most Portuguese settlers avoided the interior of Brazil, with its hostile native tribes, dense forests, and deadly animals, insects, and snakes. However, some men—driven by the desire to find gold, jewels, and native people to trade as slaves—organized expeditions into the Amazon forests that could last for months or even years. These were the *bandeirantes,* so called for the *bandeiras*, or banners, that they wore or carried with them to identify themselves. They traveled with other bandeirantes and native Amazonian people, and wore almost no clothing, like the natives.

BRASILIANI EX AMERICA
armati habitus.

This native Amazonian's full, feathered cloak is a sign of his high status.

These drawings, from a nineteenth-century atlas, show some of the pierced lip ornaments worn by Amazonian natives.

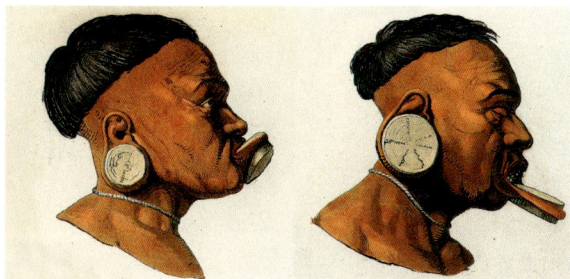

Native Americans

When the first European explorers arrived in North America in the sixteenth century, there were an estimated 1.3 million people already living there, who spoke more than two hundred different languages. The Native Americans did not have systems of writing or hieroglyphics. Instead they relied upon a strong oral tradition of storytelling and ritual reenactments to pass on their legends, history, spiritual beliefs, and cultural traditions to their descendants. As a result, much of what we know today about how the Native Americans lived and dressed comes from accounts told by the Europeans who first encountered them.

Ishtaboli

The Choctaw men loved to play ishtaboli, a stick and ball game that the French colonists renamed lacrosse. The game was so violent that the Choctaw called it "the little brother of war." The Choctaw built huge playing fields that could hold up to seven hundred ishtaboli players at one time. To play, warriors and nobles would wear loincloths with fringed belts and elaborate structures covered in egret feathers that stuck out behind them like tails. They carried long sticks made from wood with webbed ends woven from strips of deer hide.

Because verbal language was so central to the Native American cultures, many native groups that shared a common language also had similar types of housing, farming, foods, and clothing. The Algonquian tribes of North

Choctaw *ishtaboli* players dressed in loincloths, fringed belts, feathered tails, and headdresses to play the violent game.

America are so called because they all spoke a similar language, as did the many tribes known as the Iroquois.

The Native Americans developed many different styles of clothing, depending on the climate, natural resources, and geography of the region where they lived. There were too many diverse native North American cultures to be described here. Instead, this chapter concentrates on a few important groups who met the first European settlers: the Iroquois and the Algonquian tribes of the north and northeast, and the Choctaw and Chicasaw tribes of the southeast.

Natives of the Southeast

The southeast of North America is flat, warm, and humid, and it contains many thick forests, subtropical lands, and swamps that are home to a wide variety of plants and animals. Before the arrival of European settlers, it was also home to hundreds of different native tribes who fished, hunted, and farmed.

Although these tribes came from different cultural groups, the hot climate caused them to develop similarly light clothing styles and decorative body paints. These tribes included: the Cherokee, an Iroquois tribe; the Powhatans, an Algonquian tribe; and the Choctaw and the Chicasaw, who both spoke Muskogan languages.

This Native American woman wears deerskin robes decorated with symbols, and both she and her child wear beaded necklaces and hairbraids.

Necklaces and Body Paint

Men wore breechcloths and leggings made from tanned deer hides, sometimes covered with grass or leaves. Women wore fringed skirts, and sometimes shirts, made from tightly woven grass or deerskin. Occasionally, wealthier men and women wore sashes and deerskin cloaks decorated with turkey feathers, porcupine quills, beads, tree bark, and fur from bears, bisons, and small game animals.

Both men and women wore necklaces, bracelets, armbands, and ear and nose plugs made from carved shells, wooden beads, pearls, feathers, and precious, imported copper. The higher their status, the more valuable the ornaments they wore. Many people tattooed themselves with patterns inspired by nature. They also painted their bodies with red body paint made from bloodroot and oils to protect themselves from insects.

The Iroquois

The Iroquois tribes were linked by similar languages and a common way of life. They farmed corn, beans, and squash, and built longhouses in the thick forests along the east coast of America from modern North Carolina to Canada, and inland from New York to the Great Lakes.

The Iroquois made all of their clothes from the furs and skins of animals, including deer, beavers, bears, bobcats, and squirrels. They decorated their clothes with fringe at the edges, and embellishments like shells, feathers, and porcupine quills. They wore moccasins made of elk or deer hide. The Iroquois also used red, black, violet, and green body paint on special occasions, and tattooed their bodies with designs inspired by animal and other natural forms.

Men's Clothing

Most clothing was made from leather sewn with sinew cords. During the hot summers an Iroquois man often wore nothing but a loincloth made of soft deerskin. He sometimes also wore a fringed deerskin sash over his right shoulder and attached to the waist. In colder weather, men wore

jackets with long sleeves and deerskin leggings. The seams on these and other garments were sewn outward and decorated with fringe. In extremely cold weather they wore long, fur-lined robes and capes. The Iroquois shaved all of their hair except for a strip from the forehead to the back of the neck, which was greased to stick up. Iroquois sachems, or lords, wore deer-antler headdresses.

Iroquois Women

In the summer, an Iroquois woman wore only a deerskin skirt that fell to her knees or ankles. She might also wear leggings that tied just above the knee. In colder weather, women wore shirts and long fur robes. Women wore their hair long and loose. The Iroquois regarded body hair as unattractive, and both men and women plucked it. Women wore jewelry including bracelets, necklaces, and earrings made from feathers, bones, clay, copper, and shells.

Wampum

To the Iroquois, wampum was a symbolic, ritual object, exchanged during important peace and war

Iroquois man with typical dress and hairstyle.

The False Face Society

The False Face Society consisted of healers who claimed to use powerful spirits to purify Iroquois homes and heal the sick. They visited all of the households in an Iroquois village each spring and autumn, wearing masks that represented faces of the spirits. These faces might have been seen in dreams, glimpsed in the woods, or imagined by the healers. The expressions on the masks varied from humorous smiles to painful grimaces. The Iroquois carved these masks from wood and painted them, using horsehair to represent hair and metal disks and paint to represent eyes and other facial features.

pacts and treaties between tribes. Wampum consisted of a string or dense web of sinew or hemp fibers up to five inches (13 cm) thick that held decorative beads. It could be worn around the waist or over the shoulders and chest as a scarf.

The Iroquois tribes made wampum from strings of purple, white, and black shell beads that were woven in symbolic patterns into belts and girdles. The color white symbolized peace, and black meant sorrow. Purple signified seriousness, and was the most valuable color. When the European settlers came they traded glass beads for wampum with the Iroquois, and the Iroquois started to use wampum as currency for the first time.

The three white rectangles on this purple wampum belt may have symbolized an alliance.

In the winter, the Iroquois dressed in warm furs and deerskin leggings.

The Algonquians

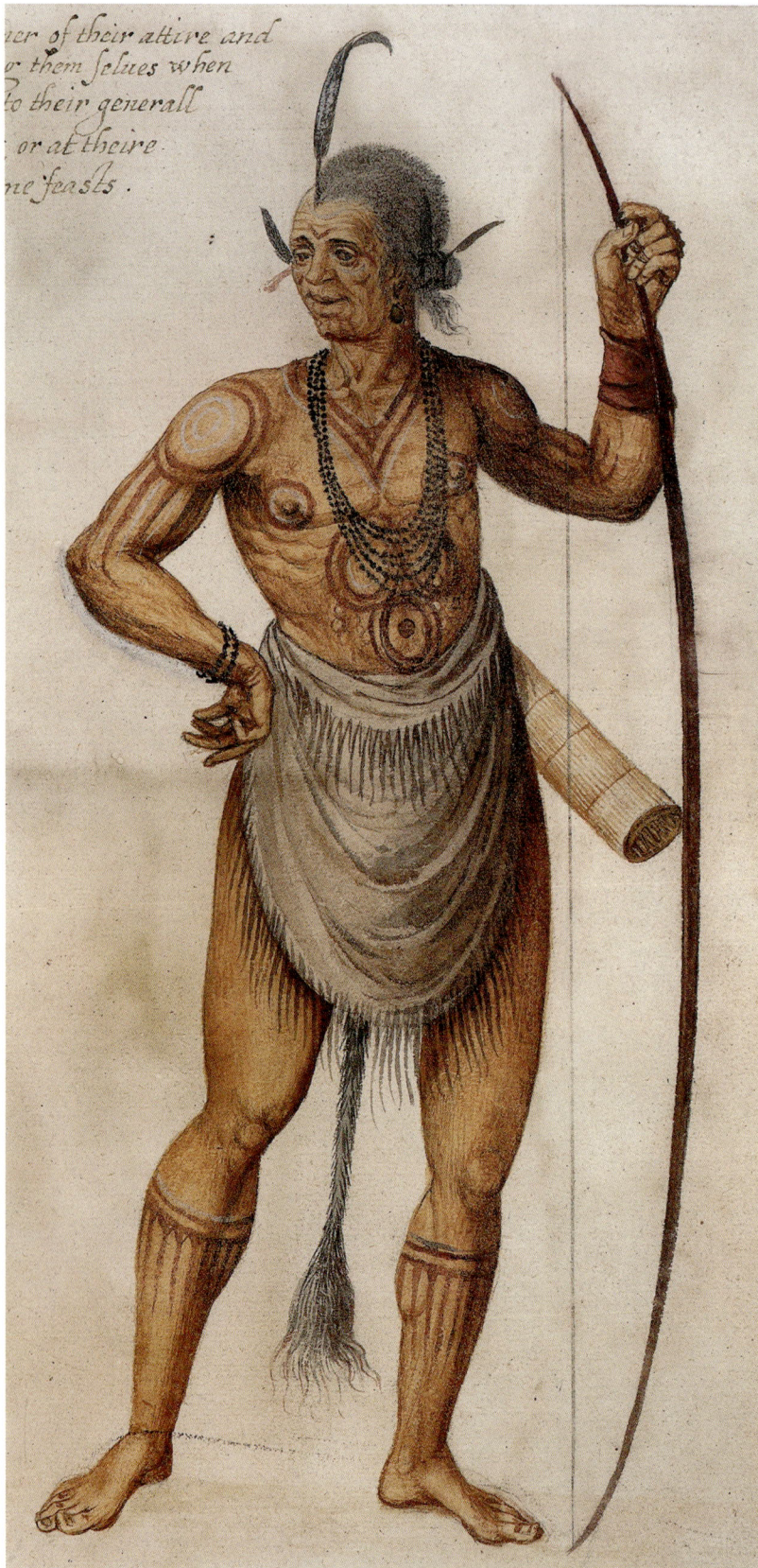

This Algonquian hunter is dressed for a special occasion in body paint, a fringed deerskin apron, a puma's tail, a long bead necklace, and feathers.

Algonquian is a term that refers to the family of languages spoken by dozens of distinct Native American tribes. These tribes lived in the woods near lakes and rivers, in areas with low hills and suitable hunting grounds, all across North America. They fished and farmed, but their main source of food was hunting. Most Algonquian tribes lived in wigwams, although some built longhouses like the Iroquois. Their clothes varied according to tribe, and they could recognize each other's tribal identities through their dress.

Algonquian tribes included: the northern Micmac, who befriended the French fur traders; the Powhatans, who encountered the Virginia colonists; and the Lenni Lenape, who met the Dutch at New Amsterdam. Another Algonquian tribe was the Wampanoag, who met the Pilgrims when they arrived at Plymouth, Massachusetts. Most of the descriptions below are based on descriptions of Wampanoag clothing.

Clothing of Hunters

The Algonquians wore clothing made from animals they had killed while hunting. Deerskin from white-tailed deer was the most common material used for clothing. Sinew from deer, moose, and elk was used to sew the hides together to create garments. In colder climates the Algonquians would wear furs from whichever animals were in their local environment, including raccoons, bears, foxes, beavers, muskrats, squirrels, and harbor seals. They decorated their clothing with porcupine quills, shell beads, feathers, bones, and stones.

Leaders and chief warriors sometimes wore long robes decorated with feathers from wild turkeys or Canada geese. Both men and women wore jewelry such as earrings, necklaces, armbands, and headbands made from antlers, stones, shells, bones, and copper. They also decorated their bodies with tattoos and body paint. As the Algonquians were keen hunters, they wore cords around their necks that held knives in sheaths. They also carried tools and supplies in deerskin pouches tied to their waists or around their necks.

Mantles and Leggings

The basic garment for an Algonquian man was a loincloth worn between the legs, tucked up under a belt tied at the waist, with the ends hanging down in front and in back. Women wore a similar but slightly longer garment. In the cold north regions, both sexes wore mantles that wrapped around their shoulders or

shirts. These were sometimes secured at the waist by a belt made from plant fibers. Algonquian women wore skirts, or sometimes dresses, with deerskin leggings underneath that tied just above the knee. Men wore long leggings that tied to their loincloths with plant fibers or sinew at the waist. Like the Iroquois, the Algonquians used wampum as a ritual offering and a prestigious garment. Algonquian children did not wear any clothing until they were ten years old.

Algonquian deerskin pouch decorated with a Thunderbird symbol.

Moccasinash

Moccasin is an Algonquian word that means "shoe." The plural of *moccasin* in Algonquian is moccasinash. Algonquian moccasins were made from deer, moose, or elk skins. Moccasins were soft-soled, low shoes constructed from a single piece of leather. This leather was fitted to the foot from underneath and sewn at the top in a central seam, which puckered around the instep. Decoration varied according to tribe and could include leather fringe, beaded floral and animal designs, or porcupine quills. Moccasins protected the wearer from the cold and helped him or her to travel over ground covered in leaves or pine needles. Algonquian people often went barefoot in the summer.

The British and French Colonies

While the Spanish and Portuguese explored and colonized South and Central America, English, Dutch, and French explorers and settlers sought new land and treasures in North America. Many explorers, searching for a Northwest Passage to India and China, landed on the east coast of North America. John Cabot was one of these men, and he claimed a large stretch of the Atlantic coast for England in 1497. Sir Walter Raleigh, a favorite of Queen Elizabeth I, attempted to set up a colony at Roanoke, Virginia, in 1585, but it soon failed. His next attempt at Jamestown, Virginia fared better. Many English people who came to North America were escaping religious persecution. They established colonies such, as Massachusetts, where they could practice their religions.

French colonists often wore fashions adopted from their homeland, such as the *justaucorps* (coat), breeches, and neckpiece worn by this man, and the fitted gown and chemise worn by his wife.

Meanwhile, the French explorer Samuel de Champlain laid claim to portions of modern Canada for France in 1608, and the explorer Henry Hudson claimed the land surrounding modern Manhattan for the Dutch in 1609. All three countries colonized and profited from the beaver fur trade.

Jamestown, Virginia

In May 1607 a group of 105 unprepared settlers—rich gentlemen unused to hard work, and laborers unskilled in farming—landed in the swampland of Virginia to found the first permanent English colony at Jamestown. Many arrived in clothing chewed by rats during the long sea

Powhatan's "Crown"

In 1608 the Virginia Company that ran Jamestown ordered the colony's leaders to make Powhatan a subject king under the overlordship of King James I, by pressing Powhatan to accept a cheap copper crown and scarlet robe. Captain John Smith recorded that he had great difficulty in getting Powhatan to wear the crown, as the chief had never seen an English royal ceremony. Three colonists eventually forced the crown onto Powhatan's head. Not having understood the ceremony, Powhatan assumed that he was still absolute ruler in his land.

journey. The Virginia climate was hot and humid, and mosquitos swarmed. Dressed in the English style, in caps, doublets or jerkins, wide breeches to the knees, stockings, and low-heeled shoes, the men suffered in the summer heat. This was followed by a bitterly cold winter, and they grew so desperate for food that they ate boots, shoes, and any remaining leather scraps.

The first women, skilled in laundering and sewing, arrived a year later. Clothing was so scarce that any laundress caught stealing clothes was whipped and sent to prison. After 1612, Jamestown finally began to thrive by trading in tobacco, capitalizing on Sir Walter Raleigh's success in making pipe-smoking fashionable in London.

Pocahontas, the Diplomat

The English settlers had chosen to establish their new colony in the middle of territory controlled by the Powhatans, a powerful Algonquian Native American tribe named for their ruler, Powhatan. In the bleak winter of 1607, Captain John Smith and nine colonists, wearing Elizabethan armor, ventured to meet Powhatan himself to trade for grain. Despite their superior arms, Smith's companions were killed by Powhatan hunters, who brought Smith before Powhatan and two hundred warriors, all with their heads painted bright red and decked with feathers. Powhatan ordered Smith's execution, but his daughter Pocahontas rescued Smith by laying her head upon his.

In 1613 Pocahontas adopted English customs, including dress, and married the settler John Rolfe. The Rolfes then journeyed to England, where Pocahontas was presented at court as a "civilized savage," dressed in stiff Jacobean attire, which hid her tattoos from King James I.

Sir Walter Raleigh (left) was renowned for his flamboyant outfits and his taste for jewel-encrusted accessories.

Ætatis suæ 21. Aº 1616

The Algonquian princess Pocahontas adopted English dress for her visit to the court of King James I in 1616.

The Fur Trade

The great demand for furs in seventeenth-century Europe spurred the explorer Samuel de Champlain to found the French colony of New France in present-day Quebec, Canada, in 1608. The colonists traded goods with the Native Americans for valuable furs and then shipped the furs back to France. New France had a tough climate with frequent heavy snow and bitter winds. The colonists soon adopted many Native American clothes that were better suited to the environment. Nevertheless, they imported most of their cloth and clothing from France. Colonial men wore cotton shirts with fitted jackets and breeches that tied at the knee. They wore a hat known as a *tapabord* with sides that folded down to protect the wearer from the wind and rain.

Beaver Hats

From the mid-sixteenth century through the mid-nineteenth century,

Cheyenne war shirt.

Buckskins

Throughout North America, men who ventured into the woods—pioneers, fur trappers, and soldiers—wore clothes made of soft, pliable deerskin or buckskin, as this was the only fabric that would not rip or snag on briars. Buckskin was used to make leggings, breeches, overalls, jackets, and moccasins. By the 1750s, yellow buckskin had become fashionable in Europe among the elite, who wore buckskin breeches and gloves made in America to go hunting and riding.

beaver fur hats were very fashionable in Europe. By the late 1500s the beaver had been hunted almost to extinction in Europe, and the demands of the hat industry drove the fur trade to North America.

Beaver fur was the best material for making felt for hats because it had interlocking barbs that produce a smooth fabric, and it held its shape even in bad weather. To make a luxuriant felt top hat, hatters took beaver wool worked into felt, dyed it with logwood, verdigris, and alder bark dye, then shaped the hat to create a smooth, cylindrical crown and upturned brim, and finally decorated it with ribbon. As this process involved imported materials and many stages, beaver fur hats were very expensive. Superstitions added to their popularity: people believed that rubbing beaver oil into the hair would improve the memory, and that wearing a beaver fur hat would cause a deaf man to regain his hearing.

Fur Trade

The French settlers traded goods for furs with the native Algonquians, Montagnais, and Hurons—enemies of the Iroquois League. Valuable furs included otter, mink, fox, bear, marten, lynx, and muskrat. Beaver furs were so in demand that beaver pelts became a form of currency. Two-thirds of the goods traded with the Native Americans were made of wool, cotton, or linen cloth, or were finished garments. The French also traded jewelry, including earrings, charms, pendants, and brooches, and colored glass and porcelain beads. One very popular trade item was a silver brooch with a hole in the center and engraved zigzag motifs.

Coureurs des Bois

The first colonists to adopt native clothing were the frontiersmen and fur trappers, particularly the *coureurs des bois,* or outsiders who lived in the woods. To survive in the forest environment they wore deerskin shirts and trousers lined with fringe, warm mittens, fur-lined coats, and moose-leather boots lined with fur. They also learned from the Native Americans how to craft large snowshoes made of bentwood and rawhide lacings that would enable them to walk quickly over the snow.

The *coureurs des bois* were the first French colonists to adopt native clothing such as fringed deerskin shirts and trousers and snowshoes.

Plymouth Colony

This woman is dressed in typical Pilgrim colonial attire.

Falling Bands

Back in England, the reign of King Charles I (1625–49) had ushered in a new style of neckwear that was less stiff and cumbersome than the large, pleated ruffs that had been so popular. The new style was called the falling band. It was made of fine lace or less expensive white linen, and had two distinct ends that hung down over the chest. Both Pilgrim men and women adopted this new style, which was much more practical for life in the American colonies.

The Pilgrims who founded Plymouth colony in 1620 were a group of English Puritans, Christians who wanted to reform the Church of England. They made their pilgrimage to America to seek religious freedom.

The Pilgrims wore clothing that was typical of English yeomen and their wives in the seventeenth century. Contrary to the popular image, they did not wear buckles on their shoes or hats, as buckles were uncommon at the time. They did not wear only black and white, but also gray, brown, red, yellow, blue, purple, and earthy green. Colors did carry significance for them, however. Black was the color of solid respectability, worn on Sundays and formal occasions. Children and servants wore blue, and reddish-brown was regarded as a color worn only in the country.

Collars and Cuffs

The basic undergarment for Pilgrim men was a loose linen shirt with long sleeves. Over this they would wear a padded doublet that buttoned down the front, with broad shoulders and long sleeves. Men sometimes wore lace or cloth collars and cuffs in white, which contrasted with dark garments. The most common style of trousers was baggy breeches to the knees, which buttoned in front. Men wore knee-length stockings of tailored cotton or wool, held up with garters. Leather shoes with low heels and low sides were common, but boots in the style of King Charles I's court were also popular. Older or

Simple falling band collars replaced the more impractical pleated ruffs of the previous era in the Plymouth colony.

This painting depicts the Pilgrims at the first Thanksgiving dinner in 1621.

more distinguished men wore full-length wool gowns over their other clothes. Men wore felt hats both inside and outside, and all men grew beards.

Petticoats and Coifs

Pilgrim women wore a linen undergarment called a shift. This had short sleeves, fastened in the front, and was tied with ribbons at the collar and cuffs. Over this, women wore stays and one or more petticoats that reached to the ankles and fastened at the waist. On top, women wore a fitted gown that tapered in at the waist, or a combination of a fitted bodice that buttoned down the front and an ankle-length skirt. The bodice might have long sleeves attached, or separate sleeves that tied to it at the shoulders. Women wore stockings and shoes similar to the men's, and aprons to protect their skirts from chores. A Pilgrim woman's hair was always worn up and pulled tightly back, covered by a linen cap called a coif.

Pilgrim Children

Blue was the most common color for children's clothing, and boys and girls dressed the same until they were seven. Their basic undergarment was a wool or linen shirt. Over this they wore a long gown wth long sleeves and a high neckline that fastened in the back. When they played outside or performed chores they wore aprons. All children wore a close-fitting cap that tied under the chin, called a biggin. A velvet cap could be worn over the biggin on formal occasions.

The Puritans

In this painting, (above) Massachusetts Governor John Winthrop performs apothecary services in his home.

The Puritans wore modest but well-tailored garments without embellishments.

The Puritan Massachusetts Bay Colony was richer than Plymouth colony, but it adhered to a stricter code of behavior that dictated specific rules on what its colonists could wear. When the colony was founded in 1630, the courtiers in Europe were wearing many jewels, velvet flourishes, silk scarves, and lace ruffles. The Puritans disliked this ostentation. The Massachusetts Bay Company, which founded the colony, supplied each man with relatively plain and practical garments. These included three suits, four shirts, four pairs of shoes, one black hat, five red knit caps, two falling bands, and a pair of gloves. The Puritans wore many shades of brown, but also black, pale blue, pale green, beige, and occasionally scarlet.

Forbidden Clothing

In 1634 the governors of Massachusetts passed a sumptuary law forbidding the colonists from making or buying any clothing with lace, gold thread, embroidery, or ruffs. Other unsuitable items included: large, decorative shoe ornaments; beaver fur hats; thick garters; perfumed gloves; showy feathered hats; and multiple rings or pearl necklaces. Another law passed in 1639 forbade poorer colonists from dressing above their station in large breeches, broad-shouldered tops, ruffles, wide boots, or silk scarves. Short sleeves and long hair worn loose were banned as signs of immorality.

The Salem Witch Trials

The colonial town of Salem, Massachusetts, was consumed by a deep fear of witchcraft in 1692. In this dangerous atmosphere the town leaders were prepared to convict women as witches on the basis of flimsy evidence. Bridget Bishop was the first woman tried in court for witchcraft, and she was accused on the basis of her beauty and her "showy costume." Her black dress with a red bodice, bordered and looped with different-colored threads, was used as evidence against her. So was her visit to the town dyer, asking him to dye "sundry pieces of lace" of "long and immodest shapes." The court searched her body for any moles or warts—regarded as marks of the devil—and when one was found, they convicted and executed her.

The Scarlet Letter

Hester Prynne, the heroine of Nathaniel Hawthorne's novel *The Scarlet Letter* (1850), was a seventeenth-century Puritan living in the Massachusetts colony. She had committed adultery, and was sentenced to wear a scarlet letter "A" on her dress forever as a symbol of her guilt. Hawthorne based his story around historical facts, including a 1694 law of Salem, Massachusetts, that forced adulterers to wear a capital letter "A" two inches long, made from different-colored cloth, stitched into the arms or backs of their clothing. In the novel, Hester Prynne embellishes her red cloth "A" with elaborate embroidery and flourishes of gold thread, and wears it on her front.

Clothes in Captivity

A war broke out between the local Wampanoag natives and the colonists in 1675. This was called Metacom's Rebellion after the Native American leader Metacom. The Wampanoags attacked colonial villages and sometimes took hostages. One hostage was Mary Rowlandson, who spent three months among the Wampanoags and wrote about her experience. She survived by making stockings, aprons, and shirts for her captors, and watched them make wampum. After Metacom had successfully raided an English village, Mary witnessed his victory dance. She later described how he dressed by combining a colonial shirt, stockings, and garters with native wampum and war paint. It was customary for victorious Wampanoags to wear their defeated enemies' clothing as a sign of triumph.

Pennsylvania

William Penn founded the colony of Pennsylvania in 1682 as a religious refuge for English, German, and Dutch Quakers. The Quaker religion treated all people as equals, regardless of race, sex, or origin, and the Quakers' clothing carried no indication of a social hierarchy.

A colonial Quaker woman wore a plain dress, apron, linen cap, and simple shoes.

In North America the Quakers' dress style distinguished them from the other colonists. Pennsylvania had no official dress code, but in 1693 William Penn instructed the colonists on clothes by writing, "The more simple and plain they are, the better. Neither unshapely, nor fantastical, and for use and decency and not for pride."

Simple Dress

Fashionable items that the Quakers rejected included cocked hats, twisted neck cloths, useless holes, buttons, and pockets, wide cuffs, excess lace, large buckles, colored linings, broad hems, and wide skirts. Instead, Quaker men wore plain shirts, breeches, and simple buckled shoes. Over this, they wore a cloak or a simple knee-length coat that buttoned down the front. Men wore wigs without excessive curls or powdering. Plain hats with broad brims were so popular with the Quakers that they became known by other colonists, derogatorily, as "broadbrims."

Quaker women wore plain dresses made of homespun fabric. Over this they wore a plain shawl that folded three times at the back of the neck. It was pinned at the shoulder and had points that hung down in the front. On their heads, Quaker women wore a white linen cap covered by a black hood. In the late-eighteenth century, they began to wear bonnets. The most popular style was a black "tunnel" bonnet with a brim that framed the face.

Hodden Gray

The Quakers of the Delaware Valley became known for their homespun, soft, gray fabric called "Hodden gray." Hodden gray was one of the first textiles to be manufactured on a large scale in America. The Quakers wore colors other than gray, however, including soft browns, earthy greens, creams, and reds. They wore black only when in mourning. During the eighteenth century the Quakers boycotted indigo dye and indigo-colored clothing because indigo was supplied through the slave trade.

William Penn

Unlike most Quakers, William Penn came from a wealthy family in England, and in his youth he wore expensive, fashionable clothing with

large, silver buckles. His father was an admiral in the British navy, and William also considered a military career. Ironically, the only authentic portrait that exists of William Penn shows him dressed in a full set of armor when he was twenty-two. A few months after he posed for this portrait, he converted to peaceful Quakerism, a religion in which men were urged not to dress in a "warlike fashion."

William Penn, the founder of Pennsylvania, encouraged the colonists to adopt simple dress.

Amish Dress

The Amish, a branch of the Mennonite religion, were another group who settled peacefully in Pennsylvania, arriving in the 1720s and 1730s. They dressed in a plain style of clothing that Amish people still wear today. Amish women wear full-length dresses made from solid-colored fabric. Over this they wear an apron, and a cape in bad weather. They do not wear jewelry. An Amish woman wears her hair in a bun on the back of her head, and covers it with a white cap if she is married, or a black one if she is single. Amish men wear dark suits with straight jackets without lapels, solid-colored shirts, broad trousers with suspenders, black socks, black shoes, and broad-brimmed hats. Amish men grow beards after they marry.

Amish people living in America today wear clothes that are similar to those worn by their colonial ancestors.

Slavery

The institution of slavery in North America began in 1619 in Jamestown, Virginia, and ended two and a half centuries later, when the Emancipation Proclamation of 1863 and subsequent laws finally abolished it. During this period, roughly 650,000 people were captured in Africa and brought on ships to the North American colonies, where they were forced into hard, unpaid labor and denied basic human rights. Around eleven million slaves were brought to the New World as a whole.

Throughout the colonies, slaves were bought and sold as chattels, and used to work on large farming plantations and perform other work. The slaveholders gave them the bare minimum of clothing required for survival, and used impersonal, uniform clothes, physical branding, and identification tags to reinforce the slaves' inhumane status.

Slave Ships

Most American slaves came from the coasts of West Africa. They had a variety of cultural backgrounds, languages, clothing, and social customs. When captured and sold into slavery, these people lost all of their possessions, including their clothing. Often the slave traders would brand their skins with hot irons, leaving permanent identification marks. A few captives kept bead necklaces or small leather items, but most were forced onto the slave trading ships naked. On the ships they were chained together and crammed into such tight conditions that they could barely move. Many died. When the survivors arrived in America, they were sold to slaveholders and given coarse garments.

Rough Clothing

Slave owners gave their slaves a minimal amount of sturdy clothing to last through each year. This clothing was made from crude textiles like rough, inexpensive woolens, hemp, or cottons. Plain white, blue, and green were the most common colors. Most male slaves who worked in the fields on plantations were given only two suits of clothing a year. These consisted of one pair of winter trousers, a pair of summer trousers, two loose shirts, and

Slave Hire Badges

From the mid-seventeenth century until the Civil War, some Southern states operated a system of slave hire badges. These badges, worn around the neck on a chain or string, identified the names and plantations of slaves who were leased out by their owners for short-term labor outside their plantations. The badges were made from copper and were most often shaped like squares or diamonds roughly two inches (5 cm) across.

12 THE NEGRO'S COMPLAINT.

THE SLAVE-SHIP.

By our blood in Afric wasted,
Ere our necks receiv'd the chain;

THE NEGRO'S COMPLAINT. 13

THE SLAVE-MARKET.

By our suff'rings, since ye brought us
To the man-degrading mart;

This book illustrates life on board a slave ship and a slave auction.

one waistcoat for warmth. Female slaves received two petticoats, two loose shifts, and a jacket without stays—a sign of inferiority. Occasionally they wore loose dresses instead. Most slave clothing fit poorly, and the shoes were so uncomfortable that many slaves chose to go barefoot. Many clothes for slaves had initials sewn into them to identify the slaves if they ran away.

The Cotton Industry

Cotton grew easily in the southern American colonies, but it was grown in only small quantities in Virginia until the end of the eighteenth century. Slaves were used to farm the raw cotton, which was then shipped to British textile producers. When the British and American textile industries started to use steam power in the late 1700s, demand for cotton yarn increased, and so did the

demand for slaves. In 1793, Eli Whitney's invention of the cotton gin, a machine that removed cotton seeds from cotton fibers, led to an even greater demand for slaves to pick raw cotton.

Slaves wore rough and uncomfortable clothing supplied by their owners.

Colonial Fashion

By the eighteenth century, the colonies along the East coast of America had become firmly established. Their towns were filled with merchants, and their countryside with farmers who grew crops for both home consumption and export. The colonists still imported most of their textiles and clothing, however, and followed English fashion trends.

Over time, the American environment influenced colonial clothing styles. The southern colonies were too hot for wigs and coats in the summer, for instance, and men in Virginia often went without them. In the dense forests of the northeast, native leather and fur clothing were more effective for exploring and hunting. Some luxury items like starched ruffles proved too fussy, stiff, or wasteful for the physical requirements of life in the colonies. Still, rich colonists continued to buy fanciful imported goods as luxuries. By the mid-eighteenth century, however, homespun colonial cloth and handmade clothing had become symbolic of the emerging, new, self-reliant country.

Protected Trade

Britain made large amounts of money by exporting fabrics and clothing to the American colonists. Tailors and seamstresses working in London produced ready-made clothes that were intended for export to America. To protect these manufacturers from competition, the British government passed laws to prohibit France and other countries from selling directly to the American colonies. The British government also passed laws to limit the quantities of cloth and clothing that the colonists could produce for themselves.

American colonists in the eighteenth century wore many English fashions.

As a result, it was often cheaper for the colonists to buy their clothing directly from England. Tailors and seamstresses living in colonial cities created some individually tailored clothes for their richest customers. More often they trimmed and sold imported waistcoats, shirts, petticoats, gloves, and other garments.

Qualities of Cloth

Linen, a light fabric, was most often used for clothes that were worn next to the skin, such as shirts, shifts, baby clothes, and summer clothing for laborers. The finest linen was soft, smooth, and bleached white.

Until the late eighteenth century, colonists grew only modest quantities of cotton. Instead, they relied upon imported British cotton or fashionable Indian cotton, which came in colorful patterns and soft, shiny chintz fabrics.
The colonists farmed few sheep, and imported most of their wool from Britain. Imported British wool ranged from rough, sturdy fabrics used for laborers' clothing to fine broadcloths used for men's suits. Wool

This fashionable fabric from the 1740s–1770s was very expensive.

that had been combed and smoothed, or worsted, could be treated to make it look like silk. Many less expensive gowns were made from worsted wool.

Silks were the most expensive fabrics, imported in small quantities from England or China. Rich colonists wore elegant silk gowns, waistcoats, and jackets, and used colored silk threads to brocade, or weave raised patterns, into garments.

Some colonial garments, such as this frock coat, were made from economical homespun fabric.

Homespun Fabric
Clothes that fit loosely over the body, such as linen nightclothes, everyday shirts, shifts, and baby garments, were sewn by women of all social classes at home. Women also knitted stockings and gloves, sewed petticoats, and embroidered decorations on cloaks and pockets for their families. Many people living in rural areas made all of their own clothing. The colonists grew small amounts of linen, cotton, and hemp to create crude, homespun fabrics that were far less valued than imported cloth. During the years leading up to the American war, however, these homespun colonial fabrics became symbolic of the colonists' growing self-sufficiency and independence.

Colonial Men

Wealthy men living in the British American colonies wore stiff, formal clothes that were similar to those worn by their counterparts back in Britain. It was a sign of privileged status for a man to wear three-piece suits made of soft fabrics, ruffled neckties, velvet shoes, powdered wigs, and other items that required care and were unsuitable for manual labor.

Life in the colonies was hard, however, and often required physical effort from every man, however rich.

Colonial men styled their heads in various wigs, tricorn hats, and linen nightcaps.

Plain, functional, and sober colonial fashions eventually replaced more flamboyant and impractical ones, as an appearance of sober trustworthiness in business became more important.

Three-Piece Suits

At the start of the eighteenth century, men wore formal three-piece suits. The suit jacket was long and grew slim at the waist, then flared outward and fell down to just below the knees. Under this a man wore a tight waistcoat, which might be embroidered in the center where the decoration could be seen. Under the waistcoat he wore a white shirt with decorative ruffles sewn into its center and sleeve cuffs. The third piece of the suit was a pair of matching knee-length breeches, worn with knitted stockings. The breeches could be lined with linen to serve as an undergarment, or worn with separate linen underpants. In the middle of the century, suit styles became slimmer, and men wore fewer ruffles, lace, and

Wigs

At the start of the seventeenth century, King Louis XIII of France went prematurely bald, and disguised this by wearing a wig. This started a fashion among upper- and middle-class men for long wigs that lasted through the eighteenth century. Wigs were made from horsehair or, more expensively, human hair. Caring for them required frequent cleaning, curling, and powdering with scented starch powder to make them white. In the colonies, short, simple wigs known as "bob" wigs were popular. Some colonial ministers preached against wig-wearing as decadent, but eventually all wealthy colonial men wore them. In the years before the American Revolution, patriotic barbers were known to deliberately mishandle the wigs of their customers who sympathized with Britain.

embroidery. By the end of the century, suits were made of dark, plain wool, and slim trousers had replaced breeches.

Neck Cloths and Tricorn Hats

Men started to wear neck cloths, a precursor of the modern necktie, in the seventeenth century. These came in a variety of styles that were elaborate at first but became simpler over time. Neck cloths were made from gathered white linen, attached to tabs that fastened to metal knobs or buckles. Wearing a starched and ruffled neck cloth showed that the wearer had the time and money needed to keep it clean.

Hats of many styles were worn by men of all classes. A popular hat was the tricorn or "cocked" hat made from felt, which had a low crown and a brim that rolled up on three sides.

Dressing Gowns

Wealthy men sometimes wore informal clothing at home, particularly before they dressed in the morning, and in the evening before they went to bed. A banyan was a long dressing gown made from linen or silk. It had long sleeves, and could have a simple standing collar. Men wore their banyans over shirts, stockings, breeches, and slippers. At home, men removed their hats and powdered wigs and wore simple linen caps instead. They slept in loose linen or cotton shirts. Poor men had to sleep in the same shirts that they wore during the day, or else sleep naked.

The sixth Lord Baltimore of Maryland wearing an expensive three-piece suit and starched shirt for this formal portrait.

Colonial Women

This beautiful colonial gown is paired with a decorative underskirt and ruffled sleeves.

Women who lived in the American colonies were judged not only by the quality of their clothing but also by their body posture and grace in movement. To obtain the ideal figure, women wore corsets from an early age. These held their backs straight, and molded their chests and waists into shape. Poor colonial women could not afford the stays, extra petticoats, and neck cloths that rich women wore as signs of good breeding. A wealthy colonial woman owned many different gowns made from rich and colorful fabrics, decorated with expensive flourishes like embroidery, ruffles, and lace.

Bodices and Stomachers

The basic item of dress for a colonial woman was a full-length gown consisting of a fitted bodice with elbow-length or full sleeves, and a skirt that fell to just above her shoes. Poor women who could not afford gowns wore separate fitted jackets that buttoned down the front over petticoats that were intended as outerwear, or bed gowns (see pages 58–9).

To decorate a gown a woman could add a stomacher—a triangular panel of stiff, ornate fabric worn between the neck and the waist that tied to the gown. She could also tie an embroidered apron around her waist to show at the lower front of the gown. Visible pockets were considered lower class, so many women carried their personal items in pouches tied with strings around their waists or in discreetly sewn pockets, hidden beneath their skirts.

Accessories

Colonial women tied their hair back and covered it with a hat, bonnet, or cap. The styles of these head coverings varied throughout the colonies according to background, religion, and class. The most common style in the English colonies was a simple white linen, or cotton cap, round in shape, that tied beneath the

Stays

The ideal body shape for an eighteenth-century colonial woman combined a straight back with a flattened front, with breasts pushed up on the chest. To achieve this shape, women wore stays, or corsets that contained stiff whalebones or—as a cheaper alternative—leather and cane. The best stays were sewn with tight stitches that held the bones in place in parallel grooves. Because women wore stays from a very young age, their bodies conformed to the ideal shape by the time they reached adulthood. Not wearing stays was disreputable. Still, they must have been uncomfortable, particularly for working women who needed to scrub, bend, and carry heavy loads.

chin with laces, or was secured in place by pins. Very expensive caps were handmade from lace and included long pieces of lace that hung down on both sides of the face. Poor women tied large cotton cloths around their heads.

Rich women wore gloves, fans, earrings, and necklaces that complemented their gowns. Jewelry was made from gold, silver, ivory, pearls, amethysts, diamonds, and other jewels. Silk shoes with leather soles were luxury items, often ordered from Britain.

Corsets and stays were made from cotton or silk and whalebones, leather, or cane.

Under the Gown

Under her gown a woman wore a basic linen undershirt called a shift, which showed only at the neck and sleeves. Shifts sometimes had decorative ruffles. Petticoats were worn under the skirts of gowns to give them shape. Some women wore several layers of petticoats under their gowns. Petticoats were made of quilted silk or, more cheaply, from wool. Most petticoats were intended as undergarments, but poor women might wear thicker petticoats covered in fabric instead of skirts.

Women often needed help to tie up their tight corsets.

Work in the Colonies

The American colonies that thrived attracted many laborers who could perform the hard work required to clear and farm the land, build houses, mill grain, and make the bricks, casks, furniture, iron tools, saddles, and other items that the colonists needed. These laborers and craftsmen came from the working and middle classes in Europe, and many of them traveled to America in order to gain land and find better lives. Women also farmed in the fields, acted as household servants, sewed, and laundered clothing. Work clothing in the colonies needed to be sturdy and flexible, and appropriately thick and warm for the bitterly cold winters, or light and loose for hot and humid summers.

Leather breeches protected working men from scratches, bites, and the cold weather.

Smocks and Leggings

Suits worn by gentlemen, with their long jackets and knee-length breeches, were too tight-fitting and awkward for strenuous physical labor. Laboring men wore short frock coats or waistcoats over loose shirts, or a combination of the two in layers, depending on the work and climate. They also wore loose smocks and handkerchiefs over their other clothes to protect them from dirt and scratches. Instead of breeches, workers wore either fitted or loose pants to the knees or tops of their shoes. If the work took them into the woods, men protected their legs from branches, thorns, and snake bites with trousers or leggings made from rough wool or leather. Men wore caps or cloths on their heads in hot weather to absorb sweat and the heat of the sun.

Bed Gowns

The working woman wore a loose, straight gown that fell to her ankles or to the floor. Called a bed gown or *manteau-de-lit,* this dress allowed her to move more easily when scrubbing laundry and carrying goods. The bed gown was fastened with pins, or held in place by an apron tied at the waist. Aprons were made from simple linen or cotton fabrics, often in checkered patterns. Over their shoulders, women tied dark cloths similar to aprons to keep themselves warm. Under their gowns, working women wore a simple linen shift, a flannel petticoat, and rough wool stockings. Despite their impracticality, women often wore leather stays underneath their gowns, if they could afford them.

Sturdy Fabrics

Manual laborers wore durable clothes of heavy linen or cotton, rough wool cloth, or cheap, homespun fabrics. In the early colonial years, homespun cloth was seen as cheap and practical, but in the late eighteenth century it became more fashionable as a sign of growing independence from Britain. Leather was considered an inexpensive and useful alternative until the late 1700s, when leather garments inspired by Native American fashions, such as moccasins and leather leggings, became fashionable as symbols of the pioneering spirit of a new nation.

American colonists balanced their need for practical clothing with their desire for attractive fashions.

Military Gear

General George Washington appreciated the practical value of Native American decrskin clothing, which was well-adapted for traveling and fighting in the American woods. During the French and Indian War (1754–63), Washington ordered uniforms for his troops that borrowed elements from native clothing. Instead of the usual European military uniform of fitted jackets, waistcoats, and tight breeches, he ordered looser, more flexible shirts and a thousand pairs of thick leather leggings to be made in Philadelphia. This uniform allowed his troops to navigate and fight in the woods more easily than their French enemies. This clothing strategy also worked well during the American Revolution.

Timeline

BCE

c. 3800 Brown and white cotton is cultivated in the Andes Mountains of Peru in South America.

c. 2500 Portable backstrap looms are first used by the people of South America to weave cloth.

c. 2400 Native Americans start to create beads from shells.

c. 800 Camelid fibers are first used in cloth by the people of South America.

CE

300s Mayan civilization develops, and the Maya develop ideals of physical beauty, including corn-shaped heads.

c.1200 The Inca Empire rises to power. The Incas wear textiles decorated with shawl pins, woven headbands, and ear plugs.

1400s The Aztecs take control of the Valley of Mexico, and wear elaborate feathered headdresses made from feathers gathered from across the Aztec Empire.

1492 Christopher Columbus lands at Hispaniola and encounters native Taino people wearing gold nose ornaments.

1517 Fernandez de Córdoba and his conquistadors encounter the Maya and trade beads, jewelry, and clothing with them. They bring Mayan gold ornaments back to Spain.

1519 The Aztec ruler Montezuma I concludes that the Spanish conquistador Hernan Cortes is the god Quetzalcoatl on the basis of his white skin, beard, and black robe.

1520s Cortes brings the first samples of cochineal dye back to Europe, where it becomes very popular with textile dyers.

1527 Spanish conquistadors first encounter the Incas and bring gold, silver, jewels, and embroidered clothing back to Spain.

1550s Beaver fur hats become fashionable in Europe.

1560s The Spanish morion helmet becomes the most popular head armor for conquistadors.

1565 Tobacco, a key American crop, is first introduced to Europe, and smoking pipes become popular as accessories soon afterward.

c.1570 The Mohawk, Cayuga, Onandaga, Oneida, and Seneca Iroquois tribes enact a peace treaty through the exchange of wampum, and form the Iroquois League.

1500–1650 The Spanish ship 181 tons of gold and 16,000 tons of silver from the Americas back to Europe.

c. 1580s The beaver has been hunted to extinction in Europe, and supply of beaver pelts shifts to North America.

1600s King Louis XIII of France goes prematurely bald and starts a fashion for wigs for men.

1616 Pocahontas travels to England and meets King James I, dressed in European clothing which hides her tattoos.

1625 King Charles I becomes king of England and starts many new fashion trends, including boots and looser neckwear.

Glossary

amulet A piece of jewelry worn as a charm or as protection against evil.

backstrap loom A loom which ties at one end to a pole and wraps at the other end around the waist of the weaver, used by native American people to weave small items.

bandeirante A Portuguese settler in colonial Brazil in the sixteenth and seventeenth centuries who explored the interior of the country.

banyan A long, loose dressing gown worn by a man.

bed gown A loose-fitting, ankle-length gown fastened with pins or held in place by an apron tied at the waist.

biggin A close-fitting cap that ties under the chin, worn by Pilgrim children.

brazilwood A tropical redwood tree native to Brazil that yields a reddish dye.

breeches Short pants that cover the body from the waist to the knees.

broadcloth A closely woven fabric with a lustrous finish, made from cotton or wool.

brocade A fabric richly ornamented with a raised design of differently colored threads.

buckskin Soft, pliable deerskin.

camelid Any animal of the camel family, including the alpaca, llama, and vicuña.

city-state A state consisting of a sovereign city and the surrounding territories.

coca A native American shrub, the leaves of which were chewed by the Native American peoples as a stimulant.

cochineal A Mexican insect that feeds on cacti and that yields a crimson substance used in dyes when crushed.

cocked hat A felt hat with a low crown and a brim that rolls up on three sides. Also known as a tricorn hat.

coif A linen cap worn by Pilgrim women to cover their hair.

conquistador A conqueror or adventurer from Spain who traveled to the Americas in the sixteenth century.

coraquenque A South American bird, the feathers of which were used in Inca royal headdresses.

coureur des bois A French colonial fur trapper who lived in the woods.

cumbi Cloth woven from alpaca or vicuña fibers, used as a diplomatic gift by Inca nobility.

doublet A close-fitting jacket worn by men in Europe during the fifteenth and sixteenth centuries.

felt A cloth made from woven wool or cotton, or a mixture of wool and fur, that is smooth but firm.

filigree Delicate, fanciful ornamental work made of twisted metal wire.

garter A band worn around the leg to hold up a stocking or a sock.

guild An organization created to control the training, working conditions, and prices for a particular trade.

harquebus A heavy gun with a long barrel that was invented in the fifteenth century.

hemp A tall, Asian plant with a tough fiber, sometimes used to make rope or cloth.

hieroglyph A picture or symbol that represents an object, idea, or sound.

hose A garment that covers the leg from the foot to the knee or to the waist.

huipil A Mayan woman's long blouse that hangs down past the waist.

indigo A plant that yields a blue dye.

ingot A piece of metal cast in a shape that is easy to store and transport.

Iroquois League A Native American confederacy consisting of the Iroquois tribes: the Cayuga, Mohawk, Oneida, Onandaga, and Seneca, and later including the Tuscarora.

ishtaboli A stick-and-ball game played by Native Americans

istle A strong fiber obtained from various tropical American plants, including the agave and yucca.

Jacobean Relating to King James I of England or to the period of his rule (1603–1625).

jade A gemstone that varies in color from white to green.

jerkin A sleeveless and collarless fitted jacket worn by Europeans in the sixteenth and seventeenth centuries.

jet A hard, black variety of coal that can be polished and used for jewelry.

labret A long piece of shell or bone inserted through the lip as an ornament.

loincloth A long piece of cloth that wraps between the legs and ties at the waist, worn as a basic garment or undergarment.

maguey Any of various tropical American agave plants, the fibers of which can be used to make rope or cloth.

mail Armor made from interlocking metal rings.

Further Information

neck stock A piece of neckwear made from gathered white linen, attached to tabs that fasten with metal knobs or buckles.

obsidian A dark volcanic glass formed by the cooling of molten lava.

ocher A natural, yellowish-orange earth used as a pigment or cosmetic by some ancient peoples.

pectoral A body ornament worn on the chest.

pendant An ornament that hangs from a piece of jewelry.

Quaker A member of the Religious Society of Friends, a Christian denomination founded in 1650 in England.

quetzal A Central and South American bird with red, white, and bright green feathers.

ruff A circular neck garment, often pleated or gathered and made of linen or muslin, worn by men and women in the sixteenth and seventeenth centuries.

sachem A lord or chief in a Native American tribe.

shift A loose shirt worn by women, often as an undergarment.

stay A corset that is stiffened with strips of bone or leather.

stomacher A triangular panel of stiff, ornate fabric worn between the corsage and the waist that ties or pins to a gown.

sumptuary law A law that restricts the luxuries that can be obtained or worn by particular people.

tapabord A French style of hat with sides that fold down to protect the wearer from the wind and rain.

tocapu A small figure repeated within a larger, rectangular geometric pattern in an Inca textile.

tricorn hat A felt hat with a low crown and a brim that rolls up on three sides. Also known as a cocked hat.

tumbaga An alloy of copper and gold.

tupu A long, straight metal pin used by an Inca woman to fasten a shawl.

vicuña A animal similar to a llama, native to the Andes Mountains of Peru.

wampum A symbolic object made of a string or web of fibers that holds decorative beads, exchanged by Native Americans during diplomatic meetings.

Adult Reference Sources

Baumgarten, Linda, *What Clothes Reveal: The Language of Clothing in Colonial and Federal America* (The Colonial Williamsburg Foundation in association with Yale University Press, 2002)

Bingham, Hiram, Lost City of the Incas (Weidenfeld & Nicholson, 2002)

Bray, Warwick, *Everyday Life of the Aztecs* (BT Batsford, 1968)

Brogan, Hugh, *The Longman History of the United States of America* (Longman Group Limited, 1985)

Davies, Nigel, *The Ancient Kingdoms of Peru* (Penguin, 1997)

Domenici, Davide, *Mexico: A Guide to the Archaeological Sites* (White Star Publishers, 2002)

Griffin-Pierce, Trudy, *Native Americans: Enduring Cultures and Traditions* (MetroBooks, 1996)

Everyman Guides: The Route of the Mayas (David Campbell Publishers, 1995)

Kolchin, Peter, *American Slavery* (HarperCollins Canada, 1993)

Mason, Antony, *Ancient Civilizations of the Americas* (BBC Worldwide Limited, 2000)

Milton, Giles, *Big Chief Elizabeth: The Adventures and Fate of the First English Colonies in America* (Farrar, Straus & Giroux, 2000)

Smith, Joseph with Francisco Vinhosa, *A History of Brazil: Politics, Economy, Society, Diplomacy* (Pearson Education Limited, 2002)

Tait, Hugh, *7000 Years of Jewellery* (British Museum Press, 1989)

Wood, Michael, *Conquistadors* (BBC Worldwide Limited, 2000)

Dress Magazine, 1991, Volume 18: "Cloth, Clothing, and Early American Social History" by Laurel Thatcher Ulrich.

Young Adult Reference Sources

Byam, Michelle, *Eyewitness Guides: Arms & Armour* (Dorling Kindersley Limited, 1988)

Deary, Terry, *Horrible Histories: The Incredible Incas* (Scholastic Children's Books, 2000)

Drew, David, Early Civilizations: Inca Life (Snapping Turtle / Ticktock Publishing, 2000)

Murdoch, David, *Eyewitness Guides: North American Indian* (Dorling Kindersley Limited, 1995)

Platt, Richard, *Eyewitness Guides: Pirate* (Dorling Kindersley Limited, 1995)

Wood, Marion, *The World of the Native Americans* (Hodder & Stoughton, 1997)

Internet Resources: Adult

Earle, Alice Morse, The Project Gutenberg eBook, *Two Centuries of Costume in America, Vol. 1* (1680-1820), E-text prepared by Charles Aldorando, Keren Vergon, Susan Skinner, and the Project Gutenberg Online Distributed Proofreading Team, 2003.

AZTEC WARRIORS AND WEAPONS
www.atlatl.com/article1.html
www.balagan.org.uk/war/1492/mexico/painting_guide_aztec.htm

BRAZIL
www.saopaulo.sp.gov.br/ingles/saopaulo/historia/colonia.htm

FUR TRADE
www.civilization.ca/hist/histe.asp
www.collectionscanada.ca/caninf
(National Library of Canada & National Archives of Canada)

INCAS
www.culturalexpeditions.com/history_peru_textiles.html
www.hartford-hwp.com/archives/41/414.html

NATIVE AMERICANS
www.civilization.ca/hist/histe.asp
www.tc.umn.edu/~mboucher/mikebouchweb/choctaw

PILGRIMS
www.pilgrimhall.org

QUAKERS
www.nanning.nildram.co.uk/quakers/history/Dress001.html

SALEM WITCH TRIALS
etext.lib.virginia.edu/salem/witchcraft
www.law.umkc.edu/faculty/projects/ftrials/salem/SAL_ACCT.htm

Internet Resources: Young Adult

AMISH
www.amish.net

AZTECS
www.ancientmexico.com

BRAZIL
www.geographia.com/brazil/brazihistory.htm

COLONIAL AND REVOLUTIONARY PERIODS
www.walika.com/sr/uniforms/uindex.htm
www.geocities.com/revwarcostume/
www.englishcountrydancing.org/colonial6.html
www.history.org

FUR TRADE
www.whiteoak.org

INCAS
www.nationalgeographic.com/channel/inca
www.theincas.com
www.pbs.org/wgbh/nova/peru/worlds/artefacts2.html

JAMESTOWN
www.vahistorical.org/storyofvirginia.htm
www.virtualjamestown.org

MAYA
ww.rutahsa.com/traje.html

NATIVE AMERICANS
1704.deerfield.history.museum/list/artifacts/ceremonial.do
www.oneida-nation.net/wampum_exhib.html
tuscaroras.com/graydeer/pages/childrenspage.htm

PIRATES
www.noquartergiven.net/
www.cindyvallar.com/buccaneers.html
www.piratehaven.org/~beej/pirates/

PLYMOUTH COLONY
www.plimoth.org
www.rootsweb.com/~mosmd/clothing.htm

SALEM WITCH TRIALS
www.nationalgeographic.com/salem
www.salemwitchmuseum.com

SLAVERY
www.afro.com/history/slavery

SPANISH COLONISTS
www.flmnh.ufl.edu/histarch/staugustine.htm
www.pem.org/embroidery_arts/overview.html
www.ucalgary.ca/applied_history/tutor/eurvoya

Index